Classroom Communication

Collected Readings
for Effective Discussion
and Questioning

by Rose Ann Neff
and Maryellen Weimer

Members of the Instructional Development Program
The Pennsylvania State University

Atwood Publishing
Madison, WI

Permissions

Contents

Preface

Is discussion one of your teaching strategies? Do you try to encourage active learning by involving students in classroom dialogue? Do you aim to cultivate critical thinking by asking thought-provoking questions? Do your discussion and questioning strategies work as well as you wish?

Most faculty find the first three questions easy; it's the last one that causes us to sigh, hesitate, and then (sometimes reluctantly) admit that we do have trouble getting students to participate in classroom interactions. Is the admission difficult because we are to blame? Some of the responsibility is ours, but we face no easy task. Today's college students are passive, very much in the receiving mode when it comes to education. You see the attitude as they recline in their desks, fold their arms, and say, with the most eloquent body language, "Okay prof, do it unto me and make it as pleasant and painless as possible."

Many of us face these passive students with very little in the way of pedagogical training or skill. We learn to teach by teaching, which is fine, but generally that makes our knowledge intuitive and less adaptable. We can't articulate the reasons why some strategies work and others don't, and we have trouble modifying what we do if we need to increase its potency and impact. But all is not against us. We have on our side intellectual curiosity, a love of learning, and a ready arena in which to apply what we learn. We communicate in our classrooms to be effective.

Moreover, good resources, ideas, and information on classroom discussion and questioning do exist. We keep running into them as we review a variety of discipline-specific pedagogical journals and other instructional sources. In fact, the widespread interest of faculty in this topic is verified by its treatment in one form or another in almost all of these publications. But most of us do not read about teaching outside of the disciplinary context, if we read about it in that context. Moreover, some of the best materials on discussion and questioning appear in well-known or easily accessible sources. That's part of the rationale for a volume like this one. More importantly, we believe faculty could increase the effectiveness of discussion and questioning in their classrooms if they availed themselves of the advice and information available in the literature. To help those interested in accomplishing that objective, we have assembled this collection of readings which, if acted upon, will improve college classroom communication.

Our objective of improving classroom communication is a noble and some would say elusive one. How do we intend to accomplish it? First, after having reviewed many potential articles, we have selected a group that effectively address current problems and practices in classroom communication. In other words, we tackle not only the problems, but their solutions. Second, we have formatted the materials in the collection to encourage faculty to *do* something about what they've read. In other words, we help bridge the gap between theory and practice. Each of our methods merits further elaboration.

Consider first what we have assembled in the collection. Faculty members are busy folks with multiple demands on their time. We need materials we can assimilate quickly; things we can read in short periods of time, maybe even during those moments when our levels of concentration are not at their peak. We need short pieces, clearly and succinctly written, not weighty tomes exploring educational heuristic and philosophical perspective. A collection of readings accommodates these needs nicely. A variety of short to medium-length pieces can be chosen. They can be arranged so that progression through them makes sense. Yet individual articles can be read independent of each other and at different times, or as the topic relates to different instructional needs and interests.

Consider this particular collection as a case in point. We separate the articles into two main sections; one on discussion, and one on questioning. We begin with the material on discussion because that seems to us the larger category. Questioning occurs as a means of precipitating further discussion and exploration of the issues. We start, quite naturally, with Peter Frederick, who considers "The Dreaded Discussion: Ten Ways to Start." This is the first in a series of pieces devoted to the "nuts and bolts" of discussion; strategies and techniques that make it happen and help to ensure that quality dialogue results. Included next is the table by William Bergquist H. and Steven R. Phillips proposing a host of different "Classroom Structures which Encourage Student Participation"; the article by William Ewens offering 18 concrete and practical suggestions for leading discussion; and finally the paper by William E. Cashin and Philip C. McKnight that not only looks at the discussion method in terms of its strengths and weaknesses, but also offers recommendations for its improvement in three different areas.

In addition to advice on using discussion, instructors also wonder about grading these classroom contributions. Edward G. Clarke proposes a method, "Grading Seminar Performance," that may stimulate other ways and means of providing feedback to students that measures their effectiveness and encourages further development of their discussion skills.

But strategies and techniques are not enough. Beverly C. Pestel writes in the September 1988 issue of the *Journal of College Science Teaching,* "Effective teaching does not depend on particular techniques, but rather the results that they engender." And so the aims and purposes, goals and objectives of classroom discussion bear further exploration. In "Designing Discussions as Group Inquiry," John C. Clarke shows us how to incorporate these aims and objectives as we plan discussions. Ralph Thompson also calls us to remember educational aims and outcomes in the questioning process. His article, "Learning to Question," effectively provides the bridge between leading discussions and posing questions in the classroom.

Knowing that our questioning techniques may not be what they could or should motivates interest in more specifics. The collection of readings ends where it begins with two pieces focusing on the "nuts and bolts" of asking and answering students' questions. Ronald Hyman offers the most complete advice in the IDEA paper on "Questioning in the College Classroom." Stephanie Goodwin and colleagues conclude with the advice and encouragement on "Planning Questions" that make the Hyman techniques and strategies even more likely to succeed.

This collection of readings can make classroom interactions more effective by offering materials devoted to expanding instructional repertoires, encouraging us to think about discussion and questions in terms of larger goals and objectives, and subjecting our current practices to research scrutiny. In other words, you're not going to make it through this collection of materials without more clearly understanding the hows and whys of classroom communication. But reading about discussion and questioning is not enough. It easily ends up being the same kind of passive learning we condemn in students. Learning about classroom communication in *theory* makes absolutely no difference if that knowledge doesn't get translated into *practice*. So our second objective is to make you do something about what you've read.

In truth, *we* cannot accomplish our second intent. If something gets done differently in a classroom tomorrow, that happens for one and *one* reason only. The faculty member teaching that class has decided to make the change. Even though faculty have what we might call "ultimate instructional prerogative," we can, by design and format of the collection, demonstrate our commitment to action. That's why this volume looks like a workbook. We'd like to encourage you to work with these materials. The margins are wide, inviting you to record your reactions, note your objections, and raise your questions. Each article concludes with a collection of questions — not designed to test whether or not you've successfully done the readings, but to explore what you intend to do about what you've read. In other words, the questions don't have answers; instead, they prompt discussion, further reflection, and analysis.

We'd also like to suggest ways the collected readings might be used so as to even further increase the likelihood of impact on instructional practice. Yes, the readings can be completed by an interested faculty member who has embarked on a self-improvement journey toward better use of classroom interaction. But that faculty member will increase the impact of the readings still further if he or she embarks on the journey with a colleague; if the two discuss what they've read, expand, elaborate and modify the ideas proposed in terms of their own instructional settings. If two heads are better than one, why not three or four heads?

The volume could be used to guide a regularly scheduled discussion group of faculty in a department interested in achieving more student involvement in learning. Or how about a department head asking a couple of seasoned veterans in the department or division to use the readings to guide a series of discussions with new faculty, teaching assistants, or part-time faculty? The volume might also be used by faculty and instructional developers who wish to encourage sustained dialogue about instructional issues. The readings and study questions can guide a series of discussions with individual faculty or small groups of them interested in the discussion method. Many more ideas might be proposed.

Classroom communication can be improved. We believe a collection of readings like this one can be used by faculty to overcome student passivity and encourage active student involvement. We invite you now to test our theory. Read, react to, and try out the ideas proposed here in your college classroom. As you do, bear in mind what Ralph Thompson observes about the importance of these endeavors. "Facts, concepts, generalizations, and theories are dull instruments unless they are honed to a sharp edge by persistent inquiry."

The editors wish to thank the publishers for their gracious permission to reprint the materials included in this collection.

READINGS ON

The Dreaded Discussion: Ten Ways to Start

by Peter Frederick

> The only privilege a student had that was worth his claiming, was that of talking to the professor, and the professor was bound to encourage it. His only difficulty on that side was to get them to talk at all. He had to devise schemes to find what they were thinking about, and induce them to risk criticism from their fellows.
>
> — Henry Adams, *The Education of Henry Adams*

The conspiracy of silence is breaking up: we are learning to talk more openly about our joys and fears as teachers, our achievements and frustrations in the classroom. As I have listened to my colleagues talk about their students and their classrooms, the one fear and frustration mentioned more than any other, as for Henry Adams, is in leading a discussion. No matter how many articles on technique we read, or workshops we attend, the dreaded discussion continues to bother us more than any other part of our daily teaching lives. Freshman seminar and discussion-based core programs continue to develop. Pressures not only to "do more discussion" but to do it well, reinforced by student evaluations and faculty development centers, do not go away. We are learning, alas, that to walk into class and hold up one's copy of the assigned text, asking, "How'd you like it?" does not necessarily guarantee an enthusiastic, rewarding discussion.

We need, first of all, to acknowledge our fears in facing discussion classes: the terror of silences, the related challenges of the shy and dominant student, the overly long dialogue between oneself and one combative student, the problems of digression and transitions, student fear of criticism, and our own fear of having to say, "I don't know." Worst of all, perhaps, is the embarrassment of realizing, usually in retrospect, that "about halfway through the period I lapsed, *again*, into lecture." I suspect that our fears about discussion (and our lapses) have a great deal to do with the issue of who controls the classroom. Although psychologically rooted, the control issue is best dealt with as a nitty-gritty practical question of how to plan and how to begin.

My first assumption is that an effective discussion, like most anything, depends upon good planning. The content goals for any given class period usually suggest employing different teaching strategies. We would like to be able to select from among many discussion possibilities with confidence. The purpose of this article is to expand the range of our options by describing very precisely several different ways of starting a discussion. Like Henry Adams, we "devise schemes" to find out what our students are thinking.

My particular schemes are guided by the following assumptions and principles about discussions:

- Because we have much to learn from each other, all must be encouraged to participate.

- It is important to devise ways in which each student has something to say, especially early in the class period.

- Students should be expected to do some (often highly structured) thinking about a text or issue before the discussion class begins.

- Students should know and feel comfortable with each other and with the teacher. As Carl Rogers and others keep reminding us, learning is aided perhaps most of all by the quality of personal relationships.

- Those relationships are enhanced by a climate of trust, support, acceptance, and respect: even "wrong" answers are legitimate.

- A student's self-image is always affected by his or her participation in discussions. Feedback, therefore, is crucial for self-esteem.

- The primary goal in any discussion is to enhance the understanding of some common topic or "text" (in the broadest sense).

- Different kinds of texts, purposes, and faculty teaching styles suggest using different kinds of discussion schemes.

My hope and expectation is that other teachers will adapt these suggestions and devise schemes for their own texts, purposes, and teaching styles.

1. Goals and Values Testing

The students are asked to pair off and decide together what they think is the primary value of the particular text for the day, and how their consideration of it meshes with course goals. "Why are we reading this?" "Why now?" After five minutes or so, invite reactions. It is not necessary to hear from each pair, but hearing from a few provides a public reality test for the teacher's course goals (Is this text serving the purpose I had hoped it would?). It also provides a mutual basis for further probing into the text. An alternative initial question for the pairs is to ask for a list of relationships (comparisons and contrasts) between this text and another, usually the most recent one. Make the instructions explicit: "identify three themes common to both texts," "suggest the two most obvious differences between the two texts," "which did you like best and why?" "make a list of as many comparisons (or contrasts) as you can in ten minutes." In this case, in order to benefit from the richness of diversity, as well as to confirm similar insights, it is probably best to check in with each pair.

2. Concrete Images

It is obvious, of course, that discussions go better when specific references are made. Yet I think we often need help remembering the content of our text. A few minutes at the beginning can guarantee that the sophisticated analysis we seek will be based on specific facts. Go around the table and ask each student to state one concrete image/scene/ event/moment from the text that stands out. No analysis is necessary — just recollections and brief description. As each student reports, the collective images are listed on the board, thus providing a visual record of selected content from the text as a backdrop to the following discussion. Usually the recall of concrete scenes prompts further recollections, and a flood of images flows from the students. A follow-up question is to invite the class to study the items on the board, and ask "what themes seem to emerge from these items?" "what connects these images?" "is there a pattern to our recollected events?" "what is missing?" This is, obviously, an inductive approach to the text. Facts precede analysis. But also, everyone gets to say something early in class and every contribution gets written down to aid our collective memory and work.

3. Generating Questions

We have our own important questions to ask about a text. And we should ask them. But students also have their questions, and they can learn to formulate better ones. Being able to ask the right questions about a particular text may be the first way of coming to terms with it. There are many ways of generating questions:

> A. Ask students ahead of time (Wednesday for Friday's class) to prepare one or two questions about their reading. One can vary the assignment by specifying different kinds of questions: open-ended, factual, clarifying, connective and relational, involving value conflicts, etc.

> B. As students walk into the classroom, ask them to write down (probably anonymously early in the term) one or two discussable questions about the text. "What questions/issues/problems do you want this group to explore in the next hour about this reading?" Hand all questions to one student (a shy one, perhaps) who, at random, selects questions for class attention. Do not expect to get through all of them, but the discussion of two or three questions usually will deal with or touch on almost every other one. Students, like all of us, ask questions they really want to answer themselves, and they will make sure their point is made somehow.

> C. Same as B, except the teacher (or a student) takes a minute or two to categorize the questions and deals with them more systematically.

> D. Ask each student to write down one or two questions (either ahead of time or at the start of class), but in this case the student owns his/her question and is in charge of leading the discussion until he/she feels there has been a satisfactory exploration of the issues. Start anywhere and go around the table. This obviously works best in smaller groups with periods longer than 50 minutes.

> E. Divide the class into pairs or small groups and charge each group to decide upon *one* salient question to put to the rest of the class.

4. Finding Illustrative Quotations

We do not often enough go to the text and read passages out loud together. Students, we are told, do not know how to read anymore. If so, they need to practice and to see modeled good old-fashioned *explication de texte*. Ask each student, either ahead of time or at the start of class, to find one or two quotations from the assigned text that he/she found particularly significant. There are many ways in which the instructions may be put: "find one quotation you especially liked and one you especially disliked." Or, "find a quotation which you think best illustrates the major thesis of the piece." Or, "select a quote you found difficult to understand." Or, "find a quotation that suggests to you the key symbol of the larger text." After a few minutes of browsing (perhaps in small groups of three to four), the students will be ready to turn to specific passages, read out loud, and discuss. Be sure to pause long enough for everyone to find the right spot in their book: "starting with the middle paragraph on page 61 — are you all with us?" Lively and illuminating discussion is guaranteed because not all students will find the same quotations to illustrate various instructions, nor, probably, will they all interpret the same passages the same way. It is during this exercise that I have had the most new insights into texts I had read many times previously. And there may be no more exciting (or modeling) experience than for students to witness their teacher discovering a new insight and going through the process of refining a previously held interpretation. "Great class today! I taught Doc Frederick something he didn't know."

5. Breaking into Smaller Groups

No matter the size of a class, 60 or six or 160 — it can always be broken down into smaller groups of four, five, eight, 15, or whatever. The purpose, quite simply, is to enable more people to say something and to generate more ideas about a text or topic. Also, groups lend themselves usually to a lively, competitive spirit, whether asked to or not. We are interested not only in the few people we are grouped with but also in "what they're doing over there." Furthermore, reticent students often feel more confident in expressing themselves in a larger group after they have practiced the point with a safer, smaller audience. There are three crucial things to consider in helping small groups work well.

First, the instructions should be utterly clear, simple, and task-oriented. Examples: "Decide together which of the brothers is the major character in the novel." "Which person in the *Iliad* best represents the qualities of a Greek hero? Which person, the same or different, best represents a hero by your standards?" "Why did the experiment fail? What would you suggest changing?" "Identify the three main themes of this text." "What is Picasso's painting saying?" "Identify three positive and three negative qualities of King David's character." "What do you think is the crucial turning point in Malcom's life?" "If you were the company treasurer (lawyer), what decision would you make?" "Generate as big a list as you can of examples of sex role stereotyping in these first two chapters." "If you were Lincoln, what would you do?" In giving these instructions, be sure to give the groups a sense of how much time they have to do their work.

Second, I believe in varying the ways in which groups are formed in order to create different-sized groups with different constituencies. Pair off ("with someone you don't know") one day; count off by fives around the room another; form groups of "about eight" around clumps of students sitting near one another on a third day.

Third, vary the ways in which groups report when reassembled. Among the variations:

- Each group reports orally, with the teacher recording results (if appropriate) on the board.

- Each group is given a piece of newsprint and felt pen upon which to record its decision, which is then posted with others around the room.

- Space is provided for each group, when ready, to write its results on the blackboard.

- Each group keeps notes on a ditto master, which the teacher runs off and distributes to everyone for continuing discussion at the next meeting.

- No reporting is necessary, or reactions are invited from several groups, but not necessarily from all of them.

Further possibilities for small groups are described in the suggestions that follow.

6. Generating Truth Statements

This exercise develops critical skills and generates a good deal of friendly rivalry among groups. The instructions to each group are to decide upon three statements known to be true about some particular issue. "It is true about slavery that ..." "We have agreed that it is true about the welfare system that ..." "It is true about international politics in the 1950s that ..." "We know it to be true about the theory of relativity that ..." And so on. I have found this strategy useful in introducing a new topic — slavery, for example — where students may think they already know a great deal but the veracity of their assumptions demands examination. The complexity and ambiguity of knowledge is clearly revealed as students present their truth statements and other students raise questions about or refute them. The purpose of the exercise is to develop some true statements, perhaps, but mostly to generate a list of questions and issues demanding further study. This provides an agenda for the unit. Sending students to the library is the usual next step, and they are quite charged up for research after the process of trying to generate truth statements.

7. Forced Debate

Although neither one of two polar sides of an issue obviously contains the whole truth, it is often desirable to force students to select one or the other of two opposite sides and to defend their choice. "Burke or Paine?" "Booker T. Washington or W.E.B. DuBois?" "Are you for or against achieving racial balance in the schools?" "Should Nora have left or stayed?" "Who had the better argument: Creon or Antigone?" "Capitalism or Socialism for developing nations?" Once students have made their choice, which may be required prior to entering the room for class that day, I ask them to sit on one side of the table or room or the other to represent their decision. Physical movement is important, and sides need to face each other. Once the students have actually, as it were, put their bodies on the line, they are more receptive to answering the question: "why have you chosen to sit where you are?" Inevitably, there may be some students who absolutely refuse (quite rightly) to choose one side or the other. If they persist, with reasons, create a space for a middle position. This adds a dimension to the debate and, as in the case of deciding between Burke and Paine or whether or not to support the French Revolution, those in the middle find out what it is like to attempt to remain neutral or undecided in heated, revolutionary times. I also invite students to feel free to change their place during a debate if they are so persuaded, which adds still another real (and sometimes chaotic) aspect to the experience.

8. Role-Playing

This is a powerful learning strategy, guaranteed to motivate and animate most students and to confuse and make nervous many. Role-playing is tricky. It can be as simple (deceptively so) as asking two members of the class to volunteer to adopt the roles of two characters from a novel at a crucial point in their relationship, discussing how they feel about it or what they should do next. Or, two students can act out the President and an advisor debating some decision, or two slaves in the quarters at night discussing whether or not to attempt to run away, or a male and female (perhaps with reversed roles) discussing affirmative action or birth control. Issues involving value conflicts, moral choices, and timeless human dilemmas related to the students' world usually work best, but role playing need not be so personal. A colleague of mine in biology creates a student panel of foundation grant evaluators, before whom other students present papers and make research proposals. Or, as students walk into class and sit down, they find a card in front of them that indicates the name of a character from a novel, or an historical personage, or even a concept. For the discussion that follows they are to *be* the role indicated on their card. Knowing this might happen is not a bad motivator to make sure students get their reading done.

Any situation involving multiple-group conflicts is appropriate for role-playing. There are many simulation games for contemporary issues in the social sciences. But for history, I like to create my own somewhat less elaborate "games," putting students into the many roles represented in some historical event or period. One of my favorites is a New England town meeting in 1779, in which a variety of groups (landed elite, yeoman farmers, Tory sympathizers, soldiers and riffraff, artisans, lawyers and ministers, etc.) are charged with drafting instructions for delegates to a state constitutional convention. Another is to challenge several groups in 1866 — defeated Confederates, southern Unionists, northern Radical Republicans, northern moderates, and Black freedmen — to develop lists of goals and strategies for accomplishing them. I play an active role, as moderator of the town meeting or as President Johnson, organizing and monitoring the interactions that follow group caucuses. The imagination can create many appropriate examples for role-playing. You have, I am sure, many ideas of your own.

But because role-playing can be traumatic for some students, and because a poorly planned or poorly monitored role-play can get out of control, I want to make a few cautionary suggestions that I have found helpful, if not crucial.

First, except for finding the cards at the beginning of class which compel playing a role, in most role-playing activities students should have some choice in how much to participate, either by deciding whether or not to volunteer or by being part of a group large enough to reduce the pressures on any one individual. Teachers should monitor carefully the unspoken signals of students who may find their role uncomfortable and intervene, often by skillfully pursuing their own role, to extricate or reduce the pressures on an actor. Generally, however, I have found role-playing to be an effective way for the normally shy student, who has said little or nothing in class, to unblock in the new role and participate more readily in conventional discussions afterward.

Second, give students some time (how much depends upon the nature of the particular role-play) to prepare themselves for their role. This might mean two days or more in order to do some research, or 15 minutes in groups to pool information, or five minutes to refresh one's memory about a character in a novel, or a couple of minutes simply to get in touch with the feelings of the character and situation.

Third, in giving instructions, the definition of roles to be played should be concrete and clear enough for students to get a handle on who they are playing, yet open enough for the expression of their own personality and interpretation. If the roles are prescribed too clearly, students merely imitate the character described (although sometimes this *is* the requirement) and have difficulty going beyond it with anything of themselves. If the roles are described too loosely, without a clear context, students will stray too far from the actual situation to be experienced and learned.

Finally — most important — in any role-play experience, as much (if not more) time should be devoted to debriefing afterward as for the exercise itself. This is when the substantive lessons of the experience are discovered, explored, and confirmed. This is when those students who may have served as observers will offer their insights and analysis of what happened. Above all, this is when the actors will need an opportunity to talk about how they felt in their roles and what they learned, both about themselves and about the substantive issues involved.

9. Non-Structured Scene-Setting

Most of the ways of starting a discussion described thus far involve a great deal of structure and direction. But inevitably, when teachers suspect that they have been dominating too much ("I blew it again — talked most of the hour!"), it is clearly time to give students an opportunity to take a discussion in *their* directions, and to do most, if not all, of the talking. The teacher, however, has a responsibility for setting the scene and getting class started. There are a variety of ways to do this, some more directive than others. Put some slides on a carousel and, without a word, show them at the beginning of class. Or, as the students walk into the classroom, plays a piece of music or a speech on a tape recorder. Or, on the board before class, write a quotation or two, or two or three questions, or a list of words or phrases or names, or even an agenda of issues to be explored. The only necessary verbal instructions are to make it clear to the students that until a defined time (perhaps the last five minutes), you, the teacher, intend to stay out of the discussion entirely. Even having said that, I have still found that I am capable of breaking my own contract and intervening or, more likely, affecting the class by non-verbal signals. I tell my students that I find it extremely difficult to stay uninvolved, and that I need their help in making sure I stay out of the discussion. They are usually happy to oblige. If possible, adopt an utterly non-evaluative observer role and take descriptive notes on the course of the discussion. To read your notes back to the students may be the most helpful feedback you can give them.

10. A Tenth Way to Start

As the term progresses, students will have experienced many different exciting ways to start a discussion, most of which, we hope, enhance their understanding of a text or issue. Once the expectation of variety has been established, there is even a legitimate place for the following strategy: stroll into class with your book, sit on the edge of the table, hold the book up, and ask: "How'd you like it?"

Although it has not been my primary purpose in this chapter to extol the many values of discussion, I assume that my bias has been implicitly clear. The key to effective retention of learning, I believe, is in owning the discovery. Emerson wrote in his journals that a wise person "must feel and teach that the best wisdom cannot be communicated (but) must be acquired by every soul for itself." My primary strategy as a teacher is to structure situations in which students have as many opportunities as possible to acquire wisdom for themselves; that is, to own the discovery of a new learning insight or connection and to express that discovery to others. In this way, their substantive learning is increased and their self-esteem is enhanced. How we plan the start of class is crucial in achieving this goal. "Hey, roomie, I now know what Emerson meant by self-reliance. What I said in class about it today was that ..." Which translated means: "Hey, I'm OK, I understand this stuff. I said something today others found helpful." Which translated means: "Class was good today: he let me talk."

For Further Reflection and Action ...

1. Have you ever experienced some of the fears in facing a discussion to which Frederick alludes on the first page of this chapter? How did you handle or cope with your fears? Were you pleased with the strategies you used to overcome your fears?

2. Do you accept Frederick's assumptions about discussion? What would you in change or add to his list of principles? Why?

3. Do you encourage students to generate their own questions about your assignments? Of the five methods suggested, which do you think lend themselves best to your discussion style and course content?

4. Consider the small group approach in your own classes. Do you adhere to the three crucial elements of small group work as advocated by Frederick? How can you improve the small group discussions?

5. How many of Frederick's structured situations for facilitating discussions have you used in your classroom? Through them, are you able to effectively allow your students to acquire their own wisdom? What can you do to enhance the learning insights of your students?

Classroom Structures Which Encourage Student Participation

William H. Bergquist and Steven R. Phillips

1. Group Discussion

Definition: Opportunity for pooling of ideas, experience, and knowledge.

When used: For majority of meetings, because of adaptability to greater group participation.

Preparation/Procedure: Preplanning to develop discussion outline. Leader encourages every member to participate by guiding the discussion.

Limitations: Practical with not more than 20 persons. Becomes disorganized without careful planning of material to be covered.

2. Buzz Groups

Definition: Allows for total participation by group members through small clusters of participants, followed by discussion involving the entire group.

When used: As a technique to get participation from every individual in the group. Highly adaptable to other group methods.

Preparation/Procedure: Prepare one or two questions on the subject to give to each group. Divide the members into small clusters of four to six. A leader is chosen to record and report pertinent ideas discussed.

Limitations: Thought must be given to the purpose and organization of groups.

3. Panel Discussion

Definition: A discussion in a conversational form among a selected group of persons with a leader, in front of an audience that joins in later.

When Used: As a technique to stimulate interest and thinking, and to provoke better discussion.

Preparation/Procedure: The leader plans with the four to eight members of the panel. The panel discusses informally without any set speeches. The leader then opens the discussion to the entire group and summarizes.

Limitations: Personality of speakers may overshadow content; vocal speaker can monopolize program.

4. Symposium Discussion

Definition: A discussion in which the topic is broken into its various phases; each part is presented — in a brief, concise speech — by an expert or person well-informed on that particular phase.

When Used: When specific information is desired.

Preparation/Procedure: Leader meets with the three or four members of the symposium and plans outline. Participants are introduced and reports are given. Group directs questions to proper symposium members, leader summarizes.

Limitations: Personality of speakers may overshadow content; vocal speaker can monopolize program.

5. Debate Discussion

Definition: A pro and con discussion of a controversial issue. Objective is to convince the audience rather than display skill in attacking the opponent.

When Used: In discussing a controversial issue on which there are fairly definite opinions in the group on both sides, to bring these differences out into the open in a friendly manner.

Preparation/Procedure: Divide the group into sides of pro and con. Each speaker should be limited to a predetermined time, followed by rebuttal if desired.

Limitations: Members are often not objective toward the subject.

6. Experience Discussion

Definition: A small or large group discussion following a report on the main point of a book, article, movie, or life experience.

When Used: To present a new point of view or to present issues that will stimulate thought and discussion.

Preparation/Procedure: Plan with others participating on how review is to be presented. Then have an open discussion on pertinent issues and points of view as experienced.

Limitations: Ability of participating members to relate to others and motivate thinking.

7. Concentric Circle

Definition: A small circle of group members form within a larger circle. The inner circle discusses a topic, while the role of those in the outside circle is to listen. The discussion is then reversed.

When Used: As a technique to stimulate interest and to provoke good discussion. This is especially good to get more response from a group that is slow in participating.

Preparation/Procedure: Leader and planning group work out questions that will be discussed by the concentric circle and then by the larger circle.

Limitations: Much thought and preparation must be given to the questions for discussion. Room with movable chairs needed.

8. Reaction Sheet

Definition: A method of reacting to ideas that you question, ideas that are new to you, or ideas that really "hit home."

When Used: As a way to get the group to react. Combine this with other methods.

Preparation/Procedure: Prepare topic and reaction sheets. Explain and distribute reaction sheets, telling students to write as they listen, watch, or read. Follow with group discussion.

Limitations: Topic should be somewhat controversial.

9. Phillips 66

Definition: This is a spontaneous method in which six people view their opinions on a topic for six minutes.

When Used: To add spice and variety to methods of presentations.

Preparation/Procedure: Define topic of discussion. Count off six people and allow six minutes for discussion. Allow for group discussion or reassignment of six people.

Limitations: Must be used somewhat flexibly.

10. Reverse Thinking

Definition: Expression of thought by thinking in reverse.

When Used: To gain an insight into others' feelings and to see another point of view.

Preparation/Procedure: Prepare topic — explain to the group the theory of reverse thinking. Combine with other methods.

Limitations: A challenge to group members.

11. Role-Playing

Definition: The spontaneous acting out of a situation or an incident by selected members of the group.

When Used: As the basis for developing clearer insights into the feelings of people and the forces in a situation that facilitate or block good human relations.

Preparation/Procedure: Choose an appropriate situation or problem. Have the group define the roles — the general characteristics to be represented by each player. Enact the scene. Observe and discuss such things as specific behavior, underlying forces, or emotional reactions.

Limitations: Group leader must be skilled so that actors will play their roles seriously, without self-consciousness.

12. Picture-Making

Definition: A way of bringing out ideas or principles on a topic by means of simple illustrations made by group members on the blackboard or large chart paper.

When used: As a technique to stimulate interest, thinking, and participation.

Preparation/Procedure: Leader and members of planning group select general principles or questions on the topic that will be suitable to illustrate. Leader divides the group into four or five sub-groups. Each sub-group is given a statement or problem to illustrate. After completing the picture-making, each group shows and explains its picture. This is followed by discussion.

Limitations: Instruction must be clear as to the value of picture-making and adequate materials must be supplied.

13. Brainstorming

Definition: Technique in creative thinking in which group members storm a problem with their brains.

When Used: To get new ideas and to release individual potentialities in thinking up ideas.

Preparation/Procedure: Leader and members of planning group select suitable problems or questions on a topic selected by the entire group. The leader explains to the group the meaning of brainstorming and the following rules:

- Judicial (critical) judgments ruled out. Criticism to be applied later.
- Quantity of ideas wanted. The more ideas, the better the chance of good ones.
- Freewheeling welcomed. The wilder the idea the better; it's easier to tame them down than to pump them up.
- Hitchhiking is legitimate. If you can improve on someone else's ideas, so much the better.

Leader rings bell when one of the above rules is violated. Recorder lists the ideas. Follow-up: type list and bring to next meeting to give to members.

Limitations: To be utilized as only a part of a class.

For Further Reflection and Action ...

1. In your past efforts at promoting classroom discussion, which of the 13 methods have you used? According to Bergquist and Phillip's chart, did you use the right procedures for the methods? Did you recognize the limitations of the methods? If not, how could you now use the method and get better discussion results?

2. Identify several new methods that look interesting and feasible for your classroom setting. Select one and plan on when you will use the method in your next unit of study. Be sure to consider its limitations and to prepare accordingly.

Teaching Using Discussion

William Ewens

In the teaching literature, "discussion" usually refers to a diverse body of teaching techniques that emphasize participation, dialogue, and two-way communication. The discussion method is one in which the instructor and a group of students consider a topic, issue, or problem and exchange information, experiences, ideas, opinions, reactions, and conclusions with one another.

For many of us in higher education, our image of college education involves more than the mere transfer of information. We want students to formulate applications of abstract principles, gain practice in logic and thinking, give us prompt feedback, and develop the appetite for further learning. In short, our images of effective teaching involve the exchange of ideas between instructor and student — the Socratic model of "Mark Hopkins and a student at two ends of a log" (Goldsmid and Wilson 1980).

Available research evidence also supports the general effectiveness of discussion techniques. Compared to the traditional lecture method, discussions elicit higher levels of reflective thinking and creative problem-solving including synthesis, application, and evaluation. There is also evidence that information learned through active discussion is generally retained better than material learned through lecture. Moreover, students often prefer to participate in discussions rather than be passive learners in a lecture (McKeachie 1978).

Summarizing the advice of educational authorities such as those listed in the references that follow, here are several strategies for teaching using discussion. Discussions vary widely across topics, cases, and instructors, and there are few general truths that apply to all teaching situations. With these qualifications in mind, here are some of the main points emphasized by experts on college teaching.

Proper Discussion Techniques

If our primary purpose as teachers is to communicate specific information, perhaps the lecture would be more successful. And if we desire extensive participation by all members of our class, perhaps we should break the class into smaller groups (dyads, triads, or larger "buzz groups") for part of the period. Classroom discussions, as typically practiced, are a middle-of-the-road teaching technique for instructors wanting moderate levels of student participation (Zander 1979).

Beginning Classroom Discussions

Discussion implies involvement. Ideally, the student and instructor collaborate to meet mutual goals. Here are some ideas for starting discussions:

- Start the discussion by posing a broad, open-ended question, one that has no obvious right or wrong answer and that will stimulate thought.
- Begin with a concrete, common experience, a newspaper story, a film, a slide, a demonstration, or a role-play.
- Analyze a specific problem. Ask students to identify all possible aspects of the topic or issue under consideration.
- Be benignly disruptive. Start the discussion with a controversy by either causing disagreement among students over an issue or by stating objectively both sides of a controversial topic (Goldsmid and Wilson 1980; Bergquist and Phillips 1975).

Eighteen Discussion Suggestions

Below are listed some further suggestions for promoting useful classroom discussions:

1. *Discussion requires preparation.* For thought-provoking issues, allow students time to be prepared. Give the questions ahead of time, or at least allow students time for reflection before they talk. Also, remember to give yourself plenty of preparation time before the class begins.

2. *Break large problems into smaller, more specific problems.* Discussions often appear disorganized because different

students are working on different parts of the problem and thus become frustrated by what seem to be irrelevant comments by other students. Thus, the teacher should break the discussion problem into smaller parts, so that all students are working on the same part of the problem at the same time. The teacher, then, attempts to keep the students aware of the discussion problem that is the current focus. For many problems, typical steps might include formulating the problem, suggesting propositions or hypotheses, getting relevant data, and evaluating alternative solutions (Maier 1963).

3. *Ask questions at different levels of abstraction.* Don't get stuck at some particular level of analysis — say, the factual level. Ask questions that require analysis, application, synthesis, and evaluation.

4. *Provide encouragement and praise for correct answers and risk-taking.* Be positive, non-judgmental, and supportive. Encourage participation by at least a smile, a verbal or non-verbal acknowledgement, or a few words of encouragement. Avoid inappropriate moralizing, preaching, threatening, warning, judging, ridiculing, or blaming.
Such practices tend to stifle effective discussion.

5. *Don't use unnecessary jargon.* Explain your terminology. Phrase your questions carefully so that they will not confuse students.

6. *Adopt the 10-second rule.* Learn to be patient and to tolerate silence. Silence, after all, can be a powerful motivator for speaking. Practice waiting as long as 8 to 10 seconds for responses to difficult and thought-provoking questions.

7. *Learn to paraphrase.* Paraphrasing, sometimes called "active listening," involves interpreting what students say, reformulating it, and presenting your interpretation back to the student in your own words. It is a method of communicating understanding and involvement that, if practiced conscientiously, involves more than merely repeating or "parroting" the student's comment (Gordon 1974).

8. *Allow students to answer.* Resist the temptation to answer your own questions.

9. *Learn students' names.* Learning their names displays your concern and lets students know you care about them as individuals. Although simple, it is one of the most important

techniques to promote discussion. If you have trouble remembering, use devices such as assigned seating or name
tags during the first two weeks to help you and the students
learn each other's names.

10. *Seat students facing one another.* Seating students in rows
may reduce discussion among them. Seat them in a circle to
promote classroom interaction.

11. *Adopt the role of trouble-shooter.* Reduce ambiguity by presenting facts or requesting necessary examples, refocusing
or redirecting the discussion, summarizing, or preventing
premature closure of the discussion.

12. *Creatively handle disagreements.* List the pros and cons of
an issue on the blackboard, allow representatives of differ-
ing points of view to debate, make people temporarily argue
from a perspective opposite from their own, or employ other
techniques to reduce destructive classroom conflict.

13. *Promote openness and honesty.* Try not to be defensive.
Don't be afraid to admit ignorance, and learn to say, "I don't
know." Use alternative views as teaching resources, and try
to promote a friendly atmosphere in the classroom.

14. *Promote student self-help.* Help students learn to evaluate
their own progress and to identify discussion problems and
barriers that have developed. Encourage good student
thought habits and help students identify their own mis-
takes.

15. *Encourage student interaction.* Encourage students to not
only ask you questions, but also to react to one another's
ideas. Promote the idea of education as a democratic en-
deavor in which people learn together. Ask students to comment on each other's remarks, and ask them to respond
directly to one another.

16. *Be a positive role model.* Actions are often more important
than words. Be careful to provide, through your actions, an-
example of your most important values.

17. *Draw on student skills.* Draw on the tremendous reservoir
of existing skills and practical life experiences already present in the class. Get individual class members to contribute
to problem areas in which they have special knowledge or experience.

18. *Summarize, summarize, summarize.* Periodically, and at the end of the class period, appraise the progress of the class by summarizing the main points of the discussion. Restate issues, point out diversions and barriers, and praise classroom successes.

References

Bergquist, William H., and Phillips, Steven R. *A Handbook for Faculty Development.* Washington, DC: The Council for the Advancement of Small Colleges 1975.

Eble, Kenneth E. "Discussion." *The Craft of Teaching.* San Francisco: Jossey-Bass 1976.

Goldsmid, Charles A., and Wilson, Everett. "Discussion." *Passing on Sociology: The Teaching of a Discipline.* Belmont, CA: Wadsworth 1980.

Gordon, Thomas. *T.E.T., Teacher Effectiveness Training.* New York: Wyden 1974.

Hill, William Fawcett. *Learning Thru Discussion.* Beverly Hills, CA: Sage Productions 1962.

McKeachie, Wilbert J. "Organizing effective discussion." *Teaching Tips: A Guidebook for the Beginning College Teacher.* 7th ed. Lexington, MA: D.C. Heath 1978.

Maier, Norman R.F. *Problem-Solving Discussions and Conferences: Leadership Methods and Skills.* New York: McGraw-Hill 1963.

Thompson, G. *Discussion Groups in University Courses: Introduction.* University of Cincinnati Faculty Resource Center 1974. Distributed by ASA Teaching Resources Center.

Zander, A. "The Discussion Period in a College Classroom." *Memo to the Faculty,* 62. Ann Arbor, MI: Center for Research on Learning and Teaching 1979.

For Further Reflection and Action ...

1. How many of Ewens' ideas for starting discussions have you used in the past month? Select one that you have not tried and plan how you can use it in your next class.

2. Do your students realize the value of student-student interaction? Is it encouraged in your classroom? Name two specific ways you encourage students to listen and respond to each other. How can you diminish your role as the only authority in the classroom?

3. Evaluate your classroom environment. Is it conducive to discussion? What can you do in your preparations to make it more appropriate for interaction?

4. After reading the 18 suggestions for promoting useful classroom discussions, rate yourself on each item. Better yet, ask a group of your students to tell you how well you are using these strategies. Which strategies could be more effectively employed in your classroom discussions?

Improving Discussions

William E. Cashin and Philip C. McKnight

> I have come to feel that the only learning which
> significantly influences behavior is self-discovered,
> self-appropriated learning.
>
> — Carl R. Rogers (*Freedom to Learn*, 153)

Although such learning can take place during a lecture, it is more
likely to occur in discussion classes where there is give and take.
Everybody knows what a discussion is, but try to find a good definition or description. In this chapter we will use "discussion" to
include a variety of teaching approaches that focus on two-way,
spoken communication between the teacher and the students, and,
more important, among the students themselves — for example,
recitation, dialogue, and guided and pure discussions.

Strengths of Discussion Approaches

As was suggested in a previous IDEA Paper on improving lectures
(Cashin 1985), what constitutes effective teaching — that is, what
best fosters learning — depends upon your instructional goals. Discussion approaches are well suited to a variety of course goals.

1. Discussions provide the instructor with *feedback about student learning*. A major limitation of lectures (one-way communication) is the lack of information about what the
   students are learning. Discussions overcome this by using
   both instructor and student questions, student comments,
   elaborations, justifications, etc. These interactions allow the
   instructor to plumb the depths of the students' understanding.

2. Discussions are appropriate for higher-order cognitive objectives: *application, analysis, synthesis, evaluation* (Bloom *et al.* 1956; Gronlund 1978). Discussions permit and encourage the student to introduce, explore, and refine ideas in ways that are impossible in a lecture.

3. Discussions are appropriate for affective objectives: *to help students develop interests and values, to change attitudes* (Krathwohl *et al.* 1964; Gronlund 1978). Discussions can do more than change minds; they can change hearts, the way we feel about an issue and appreciate it.

4. Discussions allow students to become *more active participants* in their learning. This increases their motivation to learn and makes the learning more interesting.

Weaknesses of Discussion Approaches

Like everything in life, discussions have not only advantages, but disadvantages.

1. It may be *difficult to get student participation*. First, discussions can be threatening to students. In lectures the student's ignorance can go undiscovered. To participate in a discussion means to run the risk of both being wrong and being found out. Also, there may be *peer pressure not to excel*. There are still students who prefer the "gentleman's (or gentlewoman's) C." Further, in some cultures it is considered inappropriate for the individual to stand out — for example, in some Asian countries and some Native American tribes. Other subcultures do not place a high value on intellectual achievement in general.

2. Discussions are *more time-consuming*. The pace seems slower, and not much may appear to be happening.

3. Discussions are *not well-suited to covering significant amounts of content*. As instructors, we must wrestle with the issue of how much of the content we cover versus the depth of the students' learning.

4. Effective discussions *require more forethought* than do lectures. They are not opportunities for the instructor to take a break. Yet preparation cannot ensure that the discussion will follow the anticipated direction. After a few bad experiences, the instructor may take refuge in a more predictable method — lecturing.

5. In discussions the *instructor has less control.* To some extent, we must go where the students' questions and interests take the group. We must allow the students to speak.

Recommendations

This part of the chapter will summarize recommendations regarding three aspects of discussions: improving cognitive or intellectual learning, improving the affective or interest/value aspects of learning, and increasing participation. The authors included in the Further Readings section at the end of this chapter treat most of these topics. Individual authors will be cited only where their treatment seems to be of special interest.

Cognitive Aspects

1. *Define the topic.* The topic for discussion should be relatively clear, that is, limited enough to focus the students' attention. "Real" or relevant issues rather than abstract or academic ones are more likely to engage the students. It is desirable to give students the topic a class or two before the discussion so that they may prepare. Often, assigned readings and study questions help.

2. *The instructor must be prepared.* It is our contention that an effective discussion requires much more preparation than an effective lecture. In a lecture, the instructor can decide what he or she will cover. In a discussion, you should be prepared to explore any issue reasonably related to the discussion topic. This means you must know the topic very well. It is advisable to list possible issues or questions that the students might bring up and to outline possible answers or responses and, if necessary, do some more reading or studying yourself.

3. *Use a common experience.* Discussions are likely to be more focused, and therefore more productive, if they deal with something the students have all experienced. Choosing something from the students' "real life" is one tactic. Providing a common experience by means of readings, a film, etc. is another. Ensure that the students have sufficient information to make the discussion productive — simply sharing ignorance is in no one's best interest. During the discussion you may have to provide additional information if lack of data is hindering or sidetracking the discussion.

4. *Acting as a facilitator is the instructor's primary role in a discussion.* Most of the content should be covered before the

discussion, either in previous lectures, readings, films, or other sources, including the students' experience. The following behaviors tend to be facilitative.

a. *Listen* — attend to the points the students are trying to make, not just your points. (Attend to their feelings as well as their thoughts).

b. *Observe* — pay attention not only to the content but to the group process — for example, who is responding to whom and who is typically ignored by the rest of the group.

c. *Allow for pauses and silence.* Students need to be given time to think. So we must exercise that most difficult skill for college teachers — keeping quiet. This is necessary if students are to answer complex, higher-order questions.

d. *Post and verify what individuals are saying.* Periodically take time to summarize or write on the chalkboard your understanding of the problems or positions, solutions or responses, being put forth by the students. Then check if your understanding is correct. When writing on the chalkboard, try to use simple phrases. Show relationships between ideas by using diagrams, etc.

e. *Request examples or illustrations.* Almost all writers agree that using examples helps people learn. The more complex or abstract the material becomes, the more helpful illustrations become.

f. *Encourage and recognize students' contributions.* Broad student participation in discussions enhances their value. Be especially alert to nonverbal clues that students who do not participate much have something to say: when they do, call on them. Occasionally comment positively on students' contribution, but do not do it every time. Otherwise, it becomes a dialogue between you and individual students rather than a discussion among the students.

g. *Test consensus. If everyone agrees, then there will be no discussion. Beware of premature agreement.* If the group seems to have reached a consensus, test this by paraphrasing your understanding of that agreement. Often only the talkers have agreed and there are still opposing positions to be explored.

h. *Provide a summary and/or conclusion.* By taking a few minutes throughout the discussion, or at least at the end, to summarize the main points that have been discussed, you provide the students with a sense of closure and help them remember. Making explicit any conclusions that have been reached is also very helpful if the topic will not be discussed further.

5. *Regarding questioning,* the following are some suggestions that encourage interaction among the students.

a. *Ask students for clarification* if their comments seem to you (and so probably to many others) to be incomplete or unclear.

b. *Ask students to support their opinions.* Sometimes students, especially freshmen, think it is sufficient simply to have an opinion. But in most college-level courses, one's opinion is less important than the reasons behind it. You are not so much interested in what they think as why. Make the students go beyond their initial, perhaps superficial, reactions.

c. *Use open-ended questions,* — that is, questions permitting the students to elaborate and think through their answer rather than just give a brief response, or a "yes" or "no." Use questions like "What are the causes of ...?" or, "What is your opinion about ...?"

d. *Use divergent questions,* — that is, questions to which there is no single, correct answer. Questions like "What were the causes of the American Revolution?" are both open-ended and convergent — the student is likely to respond with a set of causes generally agreed upon by historians. Questions like "What is your opinion about the greenhouse effect?"... "or capital punishment?" permit the students to talk about what they think. They can explore one position without having to cover others.

e. *Rephrase questions* if students cannot respond to your first question. Your second question can help the students focus on previous material that might be relevant, or it can draw their attention to some limitation or inconsistency in a previous response.

f. *Pause and give the students time to reflect* and think through their responses. Especially with higher-order concepts in our culture, silence is socially awkward. You may need to train your students (and yourself) to feel comfortable with silences.

6. *Possible stages to follow.* There are many paths which a discussion might productively travel. The following is one general plan:

   a. *Define the problem.* Until there is some agreement about what the problem, question, or issue is, the discussion is likely to make little progress.

   b. *Have students suggest possible solutions.* Brainstorming — having the group suggest as many solutions as possible without any discussion of their feasibility — is one approach. The group should avoid criticizing or making evaluative judgments at this point.

   c. *Collect relevant data or comments from the students* about the relative advantages and disadvantages of the proposed solutions. At this stage, the focus is still on elaboration rather than evaluation.

   d. *Evaluate the various solutions, positions, and conclusions.* Now is the time to judge, compare, weigh, and evaluate.

   e. *Decide upon a solution, position, etc.* If, at the end of the previous stage, one position clearly is better than the other alternatives, then you are already finished. But most questions have more than one "good" answer. In such cases, the group, or the various individuals, must decide which position they choose to embrace, at least for now.

Affective Aspects

Many academics tend to conceive of college as primarily, if not exclusively, an intellectual or cognitive experience. Such a conception of college ignores at least two considerations. First, individual students often bring to college feelings, interests, and values that hinder their learning or understanding of content we may consider objective. Second, college is about values at least values like logical thinking, clear expression, knowing the data or literature, appreciating the subject and being responsible for one's own work. At a more profound level, college is also about what kind of person one aspires to be, what kind of world the student wants, and what life is about. Our teaching is value-laden, and appropriately so. Discussion approaches are well-suited to many of these concerns about feelings, interests, and values; hence, this section on affective aspects of discussions is included.

7. *Know your students.* Start the discussion with something relevant to the students' interests and goals — something out of their experience.

8. *Be patient.* Discussion classes take more time to get going. Therefore, be careful not to talk too much, especially at the beginning.

9. *Be sensitive to student's feelings.* Sometimes, students suppress their negative feelings. But those feelings still remain an obstacle to learning. Sometimes, students get into arguments (vs. discussion); this does not foster learning. Sometimes, students attack the professor. Do not take it personally. You may want to get these feelings out in the open and talk about them.

10. *Challenge the students, but do not threaten them.* This can be a very difficult balance to achieve. You want to arouse the students enough to stretch themselves, but not so much that it becomes counter-productive. What makes it especially difficult is that what challenges one student may distress another. Some suggestions:

   a. *Do not question a single student for too long.* If the student cannot respond after a second, focusing question, move on to other students. Demonstrating how much an individual student does not know rarely serves a useful purpose.

   b. *Use personal anecdotes.* Using your own experiences and showing that you are human can facilitate the discussion, if done in moderation.

11. *Avoid premature agreement.* We have already talked about testing for consensus (4g above). You may wish to ask a student or group to argue against the apparent consensus. Or you may want to play devil's advocate — very carefully; avoid being so convincing that later some students will consider you to be intellectually dishonest. (See McKeachie 1986, pp. 33-34 for an extended discussion.)

12. *Deal with conflicts.* Do not ignore them. A helpful first step is to define the apparent areas of conflict. The problem may simply be cognitive misunderstanding, although often it is

not. You may want to write the pros and cons on the chalk-board, or you may want to arrange for the two sides to de-bate the issue. In some way, at least, explicitly address the conflict.

13. *Recommended instructor behaviors:*

a. *Be silent;* when in doubt, keep quiet. (See 5f above.)

b. *Hear the students out.* Concentrate on the points the stu-dents are trying to make more than the points you want to make.

c. *Inquire.* Ask the student to elaborate, clarify, expand, explain, explore, etc.

d. *Paraphrase* what a student has said, first, to check your understanding, and second, to show that you are listening. This is helpful behavior for the other students also.

e. *Be accepting* rather than judgmental or evaluative. Try to focus on the "correct" part of the student's response. Posi-tive reinforcement will foster more learning than negative reinforcement. (Eventually your grading criteria will have to be taken into consideration, and they will have an im-portant influence. See 15 below.)

Regarding Participation

The following are some suggestions about what you might do to in-crease student involvement and interaction in your discussions.

14. *Create the expectation of participation.* Arrange the seating so that it is easy for everyone to see one another (e.g., around a table or with a circle of chairs). Make the instruc-tor part of the group, e.g., not behind a desk, but seated in the same kind of chair, etc. Help students to get to know one another (e.g., have them interview someone they do not know). Get the students to talk (e.g., have them introduce the person they interviewed). Help them learn each other's name.

15. *Clarify how participation will influence grades,* and do this *early* and *clearly*.

16. *Avoid looking directly at the student speaking.* Socially, we are conditioned to look at the person who is speaking. If you, as the instructor, typically do this, the students will speak to

you, not the group. If Student B is responding to something Student A said, you might look at Student A. Also, look at the other students to see how they are reacting to the speaker. Use gestures and nods to direct the students' attention to other students, not to you. Or simply say, "Talk to him (or her)."

17. *Control excessive talkers.* For example:

    a. *Do not call on the "talkers" first.* Wait to see if someone else raises a hand or volunteers a comment.

    b. *Solicit responses from the "nontalkers."* Be alert to nonverbal cues indicating that they have something to say and call on them; "Did you want to say something ...?" or "Let's hear from some of you who haven't said anything yet."

    c. *Have the class observed by someone assigned as an observer,* then discuss who is talking, how often, to whom, etc. Often, this will make both the "talkers" and "nontalkers" modify their behavior.

    d. *Talk to the student outside of class* if all else fails.

18. *Instructor's role as group leader.* Many of the "gatekeeping" responsibilities in the group process literature are also appropriate in discussion groups.

    a. *Call the class to order.*

    b. *Help the group clarify its goals.* Even if the goals are primarily the instructor's, it helps to make them clear. In more flexible groups in which the students have a major voice in determining the goals, such clarification becomes essential.

    c. *Keep the group on track.* Sometimes this can be done by simply calling attention to the fact that the individual or group is getting off the point.

    d. *Clarify and mediate differences.* (See 12 above on dealing with conflicts.)

    e. *Summarize and draw conclusions.* (See 4h above.)

Conclusions

As with the *IDEA Paper* on improving lectures, the recommendations in this chapter are suggestions of things that may help create

and maintain an effective discussion. They are not prescriptions —
things that you *must* do. If these recommendations are helpful, use
them. If not, perhaps some of the further readings will be of help.

References and Further Readings

Note: All of the citations that follow, if they have specific page numbers listed after them, are recommended for further reading. The recommended first choice
has two asterisks after it; a single asterisk follows recommended second choices.

Barnes-McConnell, P.W. "Leading Discussions." In Ohmer Milton and associates (Eds.), *On
College Teaching: A Guide to Contemporary Practices*. San Francisco: Jossey-Bass
1978, pp.62-100.**

Bligh, Donald A., Ebrahim, G.J., Jaques, David, and Piper, David Warren. *Teaching
Students*. Devon, England: Exeter University Teaching Services 1975, pp. 146-172.

Bloom, Benjamin S., Engelhart, Max D., Furst, Edward J., Hill, W.H., and Krathwohl,
David R. *Taxonomy of Educational Objectives: The Classification of Educational
Goals. Handbook I, Cognitive Domain*. New York: David McKay 1956.

Cashin, William E. *Improving Lectures*. IDEA Paper No. 14. Manhattan, KS: Kansas State
University, Center for Faculty Evaluation and Development 1985.

Cashin, William E., Brock, Stephen C., and Owens, Richard E. *Answering and Asking
Questions: A Practical Guide for IDEA Users*. Manhattan, KS: Kansas State
University, Center for Faculty Evaluation and Development 1976.

Crow, M.L. "Teaching as an Interactive Process." In Kenneth E. Eble (Ed.), *Improving
Teaching Styles*. New Directions for Teaching and Learning, No. 1. San Francisco:
Jossey-Bass 1980. pp. 41-55.*

Davis, R.H., Frey, J.P., and Alexander, L.T. *The Discussion Method*. Guides for the
Improvement of Instruction in Higher Education, No. 6. East Lansing: Michigan State
University 1977.*

Eble, Kenneth E. *The Craft of Teaching*. San Francisco: Jossey-Bass 1976, pp. 54-65.

Fuhrmann, Barbara Schneider, and Grasha, Anthony F. *A Practical Handbook for College
Teachers*. Boston: Little, Brown 1983, pp. 141-164.

Gronlund, Norman Edward. *Stating Objectives for Classroom Instruction*. 2nd ed. New
York: Macmillan 1978.

Hyman, Ronald T. *Ways of Teaching*. 2nd ed. Philadelphia: J.B. Lippincott 1974, pp.69-186.

Krathwohl, David R., Bloom, Benjamin S., and Masia, Bertram B. (Eds.). *Taxonomy of
Educational Objectives: The Classification of Educational Goals. Handbook II,
Affective Domain*. New York: David McKay 1964.

Lowman, Joseph. *Mastering the Techniques of Teaching*. San Francisco: Jossey-Bass 1984,
pp.119-145.

McKeachie, Wilbert J. *Teaching Tips: A Guidebook for the Beginning College Teacher*. 8th
ed. Lexington MA: D.C. Heath 1986, pp. 27-52.*

McKnight, Philip C. *On Guiding (Not Leading) Discussions: A Practical Guide for IDEA
Users*. Manhattan, KS: Kansas State University, Center for Faculty Evaluation and
Development 1978.

Olmstead, Joseph A. Small-Group Instruction: Theory and Practice. Alexandria, VA:
Human Resources Organization 1974.

Rogers, Carl R. *Freedom to Learn*. Columbus, OH: Charles E. Merrill 1969.

For Further Reflection and Action ...

1. What do you hope students will know and be skilled to do after your course(s)? Is the discussion method an effective means for obtaining these objectives? In light of the strengths and weaknesses discussed, why or why not?

2. What percentage of your students actively engage in regular discussion? Are you satisfied with the proportion of students who participate in them? Are you satisfied with the quality of discussion?

3. How skilled are you in interpreting the feedback your students provide in their questions, comments, elaborations, etc.? Asked another way, what do their "discussions" tell you about your teaching?

4. Review the eight behaviors of a good facilitator. Which of these are your strengths? weaknesses? Think of a specific way to improve your facilitation skills in your next discussion.

5. How comfortable are you in dealing with the affective aspects of discussion? Are your behaviors and words consistent in expressing acceptance of your students' thoughts and feelings?

6. What techniques do you employ to start, control, and conclude a discussion? How can these be modified to improve the quality of the discussion? the atmosphere for interaction?

Grading Seminar Performance

Edward G. Clarke

Next to texts and lectures, classroom discussions and seminars are the most common approaches to teaching in American higher education (Kozma *et al.* 1978). Seminars commonly mean a small number of advanced students whose research is presented and critically reviewed by class and instructor. More generally, however, discussion techniques can be used in any course in which students are encouraged to develop personal insights in an atmosphere of reflective thinking or problem-solving (Hoover 1980). Success in seminar and discussion calls upon a wide range of verbal skills, such as speaking, listening and formulating, and responding to questions. This paper will propose an approach to evaluating these skills that is suitable to both seminars and classroom discussions.

Seminar courses are offered by virtually every college and university in the country, and research indicates that structured classroom discussions are increasingly popular with faculty members (Hoover 1980, Armstrong and Boud 1983, Wood 1979) and students (Eash and Bennet 1964). Why is this the case?

This surge is partially the result of an effort over the past ten years to clarify the goals and outcomes of a college education (McKeachie 1978). On such lists are found cognitive skills and personal qualities that are not readily stimulated either by the passive participation encouraged in the lecture hall or the solitary scholarship of the textbook. Increasingly, college educators are turning to student-centered techniques, such as discussion and seminars.

Research on the use of these approaches indicates that college teachers are correct in their hopes for the potential of seminars and class discussion (Barnes 1979, Smith 1978). While it is clear that bodies of knowledge cannot be transmitted efficiently through discussion, there is nonetheless a wide and important spectrum of outcomes for both students and faculty that this technique can promote.

For the student, there are both personal and skill goals (Kozma *et al.* 1978, McKeachie 1978). Personally, discussion techniques can affect attitude change, increase sensitivity and motivation, explore questions of values, and encourage responsibility. Discussion also can promote higher cognitive skills (integration, synthesis, and creativity), problem-solving, critical thinking, and communication (listening, questioning, etc.). The teacher also has goals consistent with a classroom discussion approach, such as fostering faculty-student relationships, developing a less authoritative teaching style, and promoting peer learning and the study of non-standard or interdisciplinary materials (Kuzirian 1980 and Smith 1978).

This chapter will (1) examine common problems encountered in using classroom discussion, particularly in seminars; (2) describe a seminar format used at Wadhams Hall Seminary-College that avoided most of the common pitfalls of these techniques; and (3) examine the use of these techniques in other institutional settings.

Problems of a Seminar Discussion Approach

Difficulties with the use of this approach can be divided into two principal areas: problems with *conducting* discussions and seminars, and problems in *evaluating* them.

Some problems in conducting these classes are student-centered (Andrews and Dietz 1982). There is often a feeling that one really cannot prepare for a discussion, since one never knows what will arise in the give and take of the conversation. Some students will not be motivated to discuss topics that they find dull or beyond their grasp. Many students are not able to participate effectively, since they enter college without the required skills of listening, speaking clearly and persuasively, etc.

Other problems are clearly more faculty-centered. Many instructors tend to dominate discussions with authoritative behavior (McKnight 1978). Many are unaware of how to run an effective discussion

(Journet and Journet 1979). Most important, few faculty members reflect on *why* they want the students to discuss a topic (Hoover 1980).

A final set of problems related to conducting discussions is rooted in the environment. For example, certain aspects of the classroom situation, such as the arrangement of chairs, can inhibit effective discussion (Kuzirian 1980).

The second major category of difficulties arises in evaluating seminar and discussion performance. Some instructors believe that evaluation is impossible due to the highly subjective nature of such assessments (Armstrong and Boud 1983). Others believe that evaluation of oral contributions is undesirable, since grading tends to increase student anxiety and thus inhibits the discussion (Haines and McKeachie 1967). Some authors assert that evaluation should focus on discussion skills exhibited during the conversations. Such process skills as listening and questioning are usually evaluated only quantitatively using charts tallying the number of instances of the desired behavior (Hoover 1980, Westcott 1982, Hansen 1983, Fisher 1975, Pendergrass and Wood 1976). Finally, some believe that qualitative evaluation of the content of discussions cannot avoid excessive subjectivity. Further, faculty members monitoring subtle qualitative variables may experience difficulty in fully participating in the class and/or modeling the desired behavior.

Fortunately, a growing body of research (Armstrong and Boud 1983) indicates that objective assessment of classroom performance is both possible and desirable. With these difficulties — conducting and evaluating — in mind, the following course design was created and tested.

A Successful Seminar Format

This format has been in use at Wadhams Hall Seminary-College for seven years in a variety of courses, such as interdisciplinary seminars on Science and Religion and Contemporary Moral Problems, and in conjunction with the *Cosmos* television series by Carl Sagan. Normally speaking, these courses enroll approximately ten upperclass students and are often team-taught. Classes meet once a week for two and one-half hours, usually at night, in a seminar room filled with lounge chairs. The courses are typically three-credit electives.

Students are informed at the outset that class participation is an important part of their grade (up to 50 percent) and that it will be evaluated each week. The goals for this participation are discussed in detail during the first class session and also at the midterm marking period. It is also pointed out that these same criteria will be used to evaluate any written work that may be required. These goals, developed over the years, are as follows:

1. *Content mastery:* The student must show evidence of an understanding of the facts, concepts, and theories presented in the assigned readings. This ability is the basis for all higher-level skills and must be made evident by classroom comments and/or responses to questions.

2. *Communication skills:* The student must be able to inform others about what he or she knows in an intelligent manner. Ideas must be communicated clearly and persuasively. Communication skills include listening to others and understanding what they have said, responding appropriately, asking questions in a clear manner, avoiding rambling discourses or class domination, using proper vocabulary pertinent to the discussion, building on the ideas of others, etc.

3. *Synthesis / integration:* Students must illuminate the connections between the material under consideration and other bodies of knowledge. For example, one could take several ideas from the readings or class discussions and combine them to produce a new perspective on an issue, or one could take outside materials (other classes, personal experiences, etc.) and combine them to create novel insights. Students who probe the interdisciplinary roots of the theories presented or who are able to view the author or the material from several viewpoints demonstrate this skill.

4. *Creativity:* Students must demonstrate that they have mastered the basic material and have gone on to produce their *own* insights. A simple repetition of ideas from the text will not suffice, nor will simply commenting on what others have said. Students must go beyond the obvious by bringing their own beliefs and imagination to bear. Creativity may be displayed by showing further implications of the material, by applying it to a new field, by finding new ways of articulating or setting the materials that produce significant insights, etc.

5. *Valuing:* The student should be able to identify the values inherent in the material studied. The underlying assumptions of the author should be identified. Furthermore, students should be able to articulate their own positions by reference

to basic underlying values. The student must not simply feel something is wrong or incorrect. He or she must be able to state why, based on some hierarchy of values. In either accepting or rejecting a position, the operative values must become explicit.

This approach can now be analyzed under the previously developed problem areas of students, faculty, environment, and evaluation.

Student Aspects

Student preparation for the course is encouraged with a written assignment before each class. Twenty-four hours before class, students submit a paragraph outlining a question or area for discussion. This assignment is not graded, but it serves several useful purposes. First, it forces the students to complete their readings well before the class, thus encouraging a more leisurely and reflective class preparation. Second, it allows the instructor to preview student insights, confusions, and omissions before class, and thus facilitates faculty preparation. Third, it ensures that every student has prepared something to say. Some questions will be simply informational: "What does the author mean by this passage?" These students can be encouraged to move to a higher cognitive level, and thus to prepare more effectively the particular skills that the professor seeks to encourage. Often, simply asking a student if the passage in question reminds her of anything from another class can encourage an integrative approach to the subject. Another assignment requires the student to state reasons for agreeing or disagreeing with the opinions expressed in the reading. This forces students to identify values implicit in the author's viewpoint and to contrast them with their own.

The students are clearly informed that the responsibility for moving the discussion rests with them, and that they should prepare suitably. This point is clear in the registration description for the course and is outlined in the first class. Faculty do not lecture, and long silences may occur if students are unprepared, but after the first few weeks students become equal to the challenge. A further technique for promoting student responsibility is the "mid-course correction." In the fifth class session, time is devoted to a discussion of the progress of the class. Student suggestions are sought, and as many as possible are implemented. Typically, students accept the goals of the class but desire some change in the practicalities, such as length of reading assignments. If the professor meet these student requests, it is as if a contract has been made between teacher and student. Complaints are reduced, and student responsibility increases.

Adequate preparation is also promoted by reading assignments. Students are informed before registration that there will be a 75-page/week reading assignment. These assignments include text materials read by all students and outside readings drawn from the interdisciplinary areas represented. If a student is taking the course for history credit, for example, then he or she will be assigned outside readings predominantly in history. Since not all students have the same outside readings each week, they are encouraged to see themselves as resource persons to the class in a particular area. Such tailoring of assignments also increases student interest in the content of the course.

Students are graded every week, not only on what they say but on how they say it, as a way of strengthening communication skills. In the first few weeks, these concerns tend to predominate the assessment. The weekly grading emphasizes to the students the serious nature of this concern, and the written evaluative comments that the students receive from the instructor(s) specify particular behaviors that need improvement. If certain problems persist, individual conferences are used to give precise instruction and advice concerning the point in question. Indeed, some of our best teaching occurs in such personal conferences occasioned by a D or an F on the previous week's performance. In contrast, the practice of issuing grades for class participation at the end of the semester holds no hope for improving the skills of the students. Frequent grading can help students identify problem areas and begin efforts to improve.

Faculty Aspects

It is clear that faculty roles are transformed in the move from the lecture hall to the seminar room. We become less a source of information and more a guide to achievement. In seminars and discussions, leadership is substituted for authority (Hoover 1980). Further, the specification of discussion goals serves to clarify what behaviors the professor needs to model. We cannot demand that students perform creatively, for example, if they do not see creative faculty members.

Our experience and the literature on college teaching indicate that certain behaviors are most important for the faculty (Hansen 1983, Journet and Journet 1979, Kuzirian 1980, McKeachie 1978, Smith 1978):

- to set goals and to evaluate behavior based on them
- to provide background information, reading lists, etc.
- to encourage, stimulate, and motivate

- to clarify, mediate, and uphold professional standards
- to summarize

Further, instructors must develop questioning skills that promote discussion and do not terminate inquiry. Such a simple technique as redirecting a question to another student can usually produce the information or insight requested (satisfying the inquirer) while at the same time allowing evaluation of the second student's response.

Faculty preparation for the seminar is enhanced in several ways. The writing assignments indicate what topics will be covered by students and what areas need to be introduced by the professor. The goals of synthesis, creativity, and valuing are the most difficult for the students to meet. Faculty preparation centers not on content but on these higher-level outcomes.

The problems from failing to consider the reason for discussion techniques are ameliorated by our specifying the previously listed five major outcomes. Although presented as student goals, they clearly are originally the goals of the faculty who designed the course, and they serve to guide their preparation for each class.

Environmental Aspects

Our classes are held in a seminar room with lounge chairs arranged in a circle. This setting allows students to see and hear each other in a natural fashion. The course is held in the evenings for a period long enough to probe the issues in depth, allowing everyone to speak at each meeting. A relaxed atmosphere can help alleviate the anxiety students have as they are asked to become more active through discussion.

Evaluation

Each class is tape-recorded, and evaluation normally takes place the next day. Our experience has been that two hours are normally sufficient to listen to the tape and to write comments for each student concerning his or her performance. This technique has several advantages. It allows the faculty member to participate in the discussion and not be distracted by in-class grading. It permits more extensive remarks based on the verbatim contributions of the students. Faculty remarks are keyed to the goals; for example, a common request is for more detailed development of ideas. In extreme cases, we have met with students before class to discuss their understanding of the material and to "prepare" the comments for the evening. It has been our experience that most students actually have creative, personal insights into the material but they do not know how to cultivate these ideas. This is a skill that can be learned, and faculty *can* teach it through discussion and careful evaluation of student performance.

The tape-recordings of class discussions often are played for students to point out particularly troublesome behavior, and they can serve as an objective record in case a dispute arises over grades at the end of the semester. (Our experience has shown, however, that such disputes are normally resolved early in the semester, after one or two weeks of unsatisfactory grades.) The tapes also permit several people to grade the student's work if the class is team-taught.

An alternate technique has each faculty member, in turn, grading during the class period. However, this prevents that instructor from being a resource to the discussion. The tape has the added advantage of allowing the faculty members to evaluate their own class contributions, thus encouraging faculty development related to the class goals. This technique has been particularly useful in encouraging faculty to limit the length of their contributions in order to maximize student participation.

Applications and Conclusions

It seems clear that the five goals specified at Wadhams Hall Seminary-College are not limited to discussion and seminar courses. On the contrary, they appear to be outcomes that are expressive of the entire liberal arts experience. Further, they need not be limited to oral performance; creativity, valuing, and the others are desirable outcomes for written work as well. As a result, future work in this area will examine the applicability of these techniques to evaluating oral comprehensive examinations, senior projects, and other forms of written work, such as term papers and essay exams.

The qualitative evaluation of seminars and classroom discussions seems to be a technique particularly suited to the current educational climate. There are two important trends active in American higher education, one proceeding from within and one from without. Internally, colleges across the nation are returning to an emphasis on the liberal arts and a strengthening of general education and core programs (Gaff 1983). Externally, funding agencies and accrediting groups are encouraging or insisting on better management and evaluation of educational programs. The approach outlined above permits the use of one of the oldest tools of the liberal arts — the seminar — while assuring that it is evaluated objectively. Such a strategy also has a high probability of success, since it requires no new equipment or facilities (computers or otherwise) or extensive retraining. Indeed, its strength appears to be its simplicity.

References

Andrews, J.D.W. and Dietz, D. "The Self-Steering Seminar," *Journal of Higher Education* 53 (1982): 552-567.

Armstrong, M. "Assessing Students' Participation in Class discussion." *Assessment in Higher Education* 3 (1978): 186-202.

Armstrong, M. and Boud, D. "Assessing Participation in Discussion: an Exploration of the Issues." *Studies in Higher Education* 8 (1983): 33-44.

Barnes, P.W. "Leading Discussions." In Milton, Ohmer (Ed.), *On College Teaching*. San Francisco: Jossey-Bass 1979, 62-100.

Carnegie Foundation for the Advancement of Teaching. *Missions of the College Curriculum: A Contemporary Review With Suggestions*. San Francisco: Jossey-Bass 1977.

Eash, M.J. and Bennet, E.M. "The Effect of Class Size on Achievement and Attitudes." *American Educational Research Journal* 1 (1964): 229-239.

Fisher, D. "An Approach to Evaluating Class Participation." *Educational Horizons* 53 (1975): 161-163.

Gaff, Jerry G. *General Education Today: A Critical Analysis of Controversies, Practices, and Reforms*. San Francisco: Jossey-Bass 1983.

Haines, D.B. and McKeachie, Wilbert J. "Cooperative Versus Competitive Discussion Methods of Teaching Introductory Psychology." *Journal of Educational Psychology* 58 (1967): 386-390.

Hansen, W.L. "Improving Classroom Discussion in Economics Courses." *The Journal of Economic Education* 14 (1983): 40-49.

Hoover, Kenneth H. *College Teaching Today: A Handbook for Postsecondary Instruction*. Boston: Allyn and Bacon 1980.

Journet, Alan R.P. and Journet, D. "Structured Discussion in Introductory Biology." *Improving College and University Teaching* 27 (1979): 167-170.

Kozma, Robert B., Belle, Lawrence W., and Williams, George W. *Instructional Techniques in Higher Education*. Englewood Cliffs: Educational Technology Publications 1978.

Kuzirian, E.E. "'Everyman His Own Historian: Socratic Inquiry for Teaching European History." *Improving College and University Teaching* 28 (1980): 124-126.

McKeachie, Wilbert J. *Teaching Tips: A Guidebook for the Beginning College Teacher*. 7th ed. Lexington, MA: D.C. Heath 1978.

McKnight, Philip C. *On Guiding (Not Leading) Discussions: A Practical Guide for IDEA Users*. Manhattan, KS: Kansas State University, Center for Faculty Evaluation and Development 1978.

Pendergrass, R. and Wood, D. "Facilitating Discussions: Skills for Teachers and Students." *The Clearing House* 49 (1976): 267-270.

Smith, I.K. "Teaching With Discussions: A Review." *Educational Technology* 18 (1978): 40-43.

Westcott, G. "Teaching and Evaluating Discussion Skills," *English Journal* 71 (1982): 76-78.

Wood, A.E. "Experiences with Small Group Tutorials." *Studies in Higher Education* 4 (1979): 203-209.

For Further Reflection and Action ...

1. Do you include discussion/participation as part of your grading system? If so, what criteria do you use to determine each student's participation grade? Do you share the criteria with students? In class? On the syllabus? Do these criteria require objective or subjective assessment?

2. Perhaps it is not feasible for you to evaluate each student's participation on a daily or weekly basis. However, given Clarke's suggestions, how might you emphasize discussion/participation to better promote student preparation and responsibility for classroom dialogue?

3. Besides using a tape recorder to review a classroom discussion, can you think of other innovative ways to aid in the evaluation process? Could you develop an instrument or some other evaluation tool?

Designing Discussions as Group Inquiry

John H. Clarke

None of us likes to see a class discussion go flat. Silence falls. Discomfort clouds the room. Fearing the awkwardness of silence, we resort to other teaching techniques, predominantly the lecture method (Clarke 1987). Happy to escape oppressive silence, our students bend quietly to their notebooks. In turning to our own knowledge to fill the void, we deprive our students of a chance to practice inquiry within our disciplines. By planning discussions as models of inquiry, we can engage students in examinations of content that also emphasize the kind of thinking we espouse (Schwartz 1980).

When concept development, creative thinking, critical thinking, or problem-solving are the goals of teaching, research favors discussion over lecture/demonstration techniques (McKeachie 1986, Bernstein 1976). Students respect an enthusiastic and accurate explanation of content, but their personal involvement may be the key to higher order learning (Astin 1984). College instructors can design discussion classes so that students use the concepts and processes of the discipline to evaluate facts and move toward reliable conclusions.

Discussion as a Cycle of Inquiry

Every good discussion is an investigation, conducted by a group of people who see the importance of seeking answers to an important problem. For a discussion to work, students must become aware of some unresolved difficulty in the content. They must feel the pressure of their own need to know. They must have access to the conceptual tools of the discipline, the terminology, the methodology, and the logical framework used to solve problems. They must agree on the sources of factual information related to the issue. Most of all, they must be led to see that their own management of the issues, concepts, facts, and interpretations is the real work of learning at the college level.

Like most investigations, discussions prove effective when they are designed to follow predictable and logical steps. Figure 1 represents a general format for inquiry that can guide the process of planning active discussions. The inquiry cycle, like its relatives in the scientific method, has four definable phases, each of which contributes to the solution of a clearly defined problem or issue.

The first phase, concept development, simply raises an issue of general importance and introduces concepts from the discipline that may be related. The second phase, concept clarification, further defines the issue and introduces procedures for exploring relationships among the concepts. The third phase, factual verification, tests the concepts or procedures against some defined array of facts from assigned reading, observation, or the lab bench. The fourth phase, interpretation and analysis, draws interpretations of fact into a general explanation that clarifies the original issue or solves the original problem. A class discussion is most often successful when it has moved through all four phases, but as long as the issue is clear in advance, it can begin anywhere on the cycle.

As an aid in planning discussion, the inquiry cycle lays a clear track through the unruly forest of a fifty-minute period, letting the instructor guide the process and students tangle with the content. The following paragraphs describe ways to prepare for the discussion in each phase of the inquiry cycle, beginning with

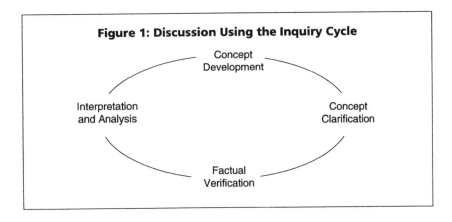

Figure 1: Discussion Using the Inquiry Cycle

concept development as a relatively safe and conventional point of departure.

Concept Development Phase: Creating Tension around Ideas

Write on a transparency or handout a guiding question that defines the dominant problem and ask students to try initial answers. Students need to have a purpose for inquiry strong enough to draw them through a class period. Instructors need to be able to pull the group back to the purpose when a discussion has ranged too widely.

In general discussion, create a list of concepts from the discipline that pertain to the problem. With a list of relevant concepts available, the teacher can ask students to define the concepts separately, to relate them to the original problem or to their own experience.

Require a three-minute "free write" on the issue or problem and use student writing to begin discussion. Students need to gather up what they know already in order to proceed further in learning. Once they have written what they know or believe, further questions and concerns will arise (Fulwiler 1987). When all students have written something about the issue, the teacher is assured of having a basis for discussion.

Concept Clarification Phase: Seeking Causal Relationships

Even with the concepts clearly defined, students need a chance to discover the relationships among the concepts, the processes producing the problem, and the procedures used to manage information or intervene in a problem area.

Describe in writing the problem students will face during the class, emphasizing its origins and its implications. Students may need to understand the nature of the problem they face before they investigate the evidence. They also need to see that the teacher has invested energy in the problem and shows genuine commitment to its solution. Tension is essential to class discussions. Focusing on the unknown, or on apparent contradictions, a paradox, or an imbedded dilemma, stirs student curiosity. But it will also stir differences of opinion that can drive the discussion.

Ask students to develop a diagrammatic representation showing the relationships among the concepts. Web diagrams linking the concepts, Venn diagrams showing the overlap of the concepts, and process diagrams showing causal links all can promote discrimination and understanding. To encourage discussion, a teacher can gain greater effect by asking groups of two or three students to define the relationship among concepts in a diagram form, an approach that breaks the ice of early silence.

Create a short demonstration of the problem as it actually appears in a real setting. Short films, newspaper articles, short lab demonstrations and photos all assure students that they are dealing with concepts that are actually affecting human experience. In many courses, the text is a reservoir of demonstration material, any part of which can focus student attention on the main issue or problem. Students see events differently. They also use different concepts to explain what they see.

Verification Phase: Scanning the Factual Base

As differences of opinion emerge, students will almost automatically turn to the facts to support their own ideas. Lines of poetry, historical dates, scientific findings, mathematical constructions, statistics, and direct quotations all are factual material forming the base of the disciplines. To promote discussion, the teacher's role is not to present the facts, but to lead students through a search for meaning in the relationship of facts, introducing disruptive facts if the discussion tends toward early foreclosure.

Ask students to search the text for factual evidence that helps clarify the concepts of a problem. Most college students do not read with the purpose of solving a problem. Their recall of most reading remains blurred until they approach what they have read with a distinct purpose. In two or three minutes, all students can locate enough factual material to bolster their own convictions. In the same period, a group of 20 can locate an impressive foundation of facts, many of which will appear to conflict, to imply larger issues, or to raise new questions. Although "fact finding" interrupts the flow of discussion, it also supplies fresh energy to a flagging or circular investigation and reinforces the academic convention of testing arguments against the evidence.

Prepare a "fact list" from the text or other sources that reflects the complexity of the issue at hand. While a text is designed to be comprehensive, a teacher-developed fact sheet can be designed to reflect confounding inconsistencies in the factual base. Unless the facts all line up behind a single set of propositions, which is not true at the problem edge of most disciplines, discussion becomes a vehicle for weighing the evidence and practicing logical discourse.

Prepare a case study, role-playing situation, or stimulation that requires evaluation of essential facts. A case study tells a factual story within a problem area and then asks students to propose solutions. Role-playing asks students to accept certain factual conditions as given and then work toward new solutions to the problem. Simulations set up situations in which certain forces are presumed to have influence and then slowly introduce new events or "facts." All three techniques encourage involvement and creativity on the part of participating students.

Analysis Phase:
From Understanding to Answers

For students to leave the room with a clear sense of what they learned, they should see how their own participation contributed to a larger understanding of the problem at hand, and also that their efforts left important questions unanswered. If possible, they should be able to perceive in retrospect the process of their investigation, how it drove toward purpose, how it depended on assumptions embedded in concepts, how the perception of relationship and gathering of facts struggled with personal opinion, and, most important, how the process drew them closer to reliable answers than they were at the beginning.

Ask students to free-write conclusions that reconcile what they have thought and what they have heard (post-writing). Students need an opportunity to draw concepts, relationships, facts, and interpretations of fact into a meaningful unity, particularly if a discussion has caught fire and ranged widely. A teacher can use post-writing from a class period to derive general conclusions for that period, putting the compiled record on the board or transparency. Over the period of a semester or more, a journal of student "pre-" and "post-" writing creates an important record of learning within any discussion-based course. At the end of a course, Fulwiler (1987) recommends asking students to put subtitles on each entry, a table of contents up front, and a cover on the whole journal for submission toward a course grade.

Ask students in groups of two or three to develop solutions to the problem originally defined as the focus of discussion. Working in groups of two or three makes it even more difficult to leap past the problems arising in discussion to settle on some easy answer. The teacher should ask for consensus among group members, squeezing student conclusions toward parsimony. Solutions from each group, written on the board, can reemphasize the struggle to agree on answers to the problems that really matter in a discipline. It is not unusual for a wrap-up group to generate a further list of questions, rather than a catalog of assertions.

Wrap it up yourself. After 50 minutes of self-restraint, a teacher with ideas and beliefs of his or her own can build up quite a head of steam. Concurrently, students struggling with uneasy answers may need reassurance that progress is possible and that others are struggling with the same issues. References to specific contributions from the class, verified in theory or research, can do a great deal to ensure that students remain willing to take the risk of discussion-based learning.

Keeping Heat under a Discussion

Some hints may help return responsibility for learning to the intended learners.

- Make a visible display of keeping a written record of students' ideas, questions, and factual contributions.
- Use the record to tie student contributions together, to point out differences, or to wrap up the discussion.
- Convert student questions to statements and ask for other opinions.
- Convert student opinions to questions for the quiet or withdrawn students.
- Deflect questions of interpretation to other members of the group.
- In response to student assertions, ask for examples from others.
- Ask questions that require inference, prediction, analogy, or synthesis of divergent ideas.
- If the class looks blank, reframe the last student response as a new question or assertion.
- Tag important assertions or questions with the student name: e.g., The Fred Hypothesis or The Virginia Theorem or The Beth Disclaimer, using them as hinge points for further discussion.

Silence Is Active

It is the instructor's responsibility to guide the process of inquiry toward reliable conclusions, usually by asking questions (see Figure 2). Initially, a class may decide that it wants the teacher to remain responsible for all words issued during a class period. If the problem and purpose of discussion are clear, however, silence may represent

---

Figure 2: Questions Driving the Inquiry Cycle

Problem or issue: What are the intellectual foundations for the form of government implied by the Declaration of Independence?

Concept Development

Guiding question: Looking at Jefferson's prologue, what words suggest the intellectual foundations of the Declaration?

Concept list: Do you think "laws of nature," "God's laws," or the "opinions of mankind" were most influential in the move toward independence?

Free-write: Why did Jefferson write the Declaration of Independence?

Concept Clarification

Implications: Can you think of instances in which life, liberty, and the pursuit of happiness are mutually exclusive?

Representation: If independence was Jefferson's purpose, diagram all the reasons listed in the prologue as they contributed to the Declaration.

Demonstration: What would happen if Alaska published the Declaration tomorrow, proclaiming liberty?

Verification of Facts

Text search: Can you identify in Jefferson's list of complaints against the king primary evidence of "usurpations"?

Fact list: Select five "complaints" that are really the basis for independence.

Case study: Acting as King George, eliminate five conditions in the Colonies in order to prevent war.

Interpretation and Analysis

Post-write: What is the relationship between the list of complaints in the Declaration and the initial arguments for independence?

Group summary: What ideas played the most influential role in moving a people toward independence?

active reflection rather than passive resistance. If the concepts are available, quiet may allow students to look for relationships. If the factual base is defined, a pause may indicate that evidence is lying on the scales of the mind.

Few reliable conclusions come quickly. Learning to wait is the central skill in discussion-based teaching. When practiced at the right moments, waiting can evoke satisfying responses. All of these techniques, if used consistently and with foresight, can result in thoughtful inquiry and lively discussions.

References

Astin, Alexander. "Student Involvement: A Developmental Theory for Higher Education." *Journal of College Student Personnel,* 25 (1984), 297-308.

Bernstein, H. *Manual for Teaching.* Ithaca, NY: Cornell University Press 1976.

Clarke, John H. "Building a Lecture That Works." *College Teaching* (Spring 1987), 35:2.

Eble, Kenneth E. *The Craft of Teaching.* San Francisco: Jossey-Bass 1976.

Fulwiler, Toby. *Teaching With Writing.* Upper Montclair, NJ: Boynton/Cook 1987.

McKeachie, Wilbert J. *Teaching Tips: A Guidebook for the Beginning Teacher.* 8th ed. Lexington, MA: Heath 1986.

Schwartz, W. "Education in the Classroom." *The Journal of Higher Education* (May/June 1980), 51:3:235- 254.

For Further Reflection and Action ...

1. Do you and your students realize that a good discussion is an investigation of some important problem? Think about your last classroom discussion. Can you identify the main discussion problem or issue? Could your students?

2. Study Clarke's phases of the inquiry cycle. Apply the cycle to your next discussion by developing each phase according to his suggestions.

3. How do your inquiry questions compare to those in Figure 2? Do you feel that your questions have adequately explored the problem or issue? For your particular discipline, are there any activities that you would add to or delete from Clarke's cycle?

4. Evaluate the periods of silence that follow a question. Are the students actively reflecting or passively resisting? After a question, is there enough wait-time for the students to actually think and formulate a response?

5. Who answers the questions? Is it always the same students? Do the others rely on them to do all of the thinking? How might more students be encouraged to provide answers?

READINGS ON

Questioning

Learning to Question

Ralph Thompson

The cutting edge of knowledge is not in the *known* but in the *unknown*, not in *knowing* but in *questioning*. Facts, concepts, generalizations, and theories are dull instruments unless they are honed to a sharp edge by persistent inquiry about the unknown. And yet the bulk of college graduates do little questioning. Even those who profess unusual acquaintance with the methods of science — where questioning is of the essence — are often afflicted with deficits in their ability to ask pertinent questions. Too frequently, their inquiry is dulled from having learned the canned questions posed for them by others or from having become victims of a system of questions beyond which they cannot proceed. Indeed, college graduates generally have not learned how to *learn*, insofar as questioning is the essence of that process.

How does one account for this shortcoming of our educational system? Anyone who is a product of our colleges and universities, indeed of our public schools, can offer an answer — too much emphasis upon the *didactic* and *deductive* approaches to instruction and too little upon the *hypothetical* and *inductive*; too much attention to *answers* and too little attention to *questions*; too much *passive* and *regulated* thinking and too little *active* and *reflective* thinking; too much *input* and too little *output*.

College instructors properly affirm that the explosion of knowledge has complicated their work. The content that many of them now select consists of the explication of basic concepts, generalizations, and theories rather than the memoriter marshaling of facts. Theirs is a *systems* approach rather than a *data* approach. Surely the systems approach is an advance over the higgledy-piggledy content arrangement of previous curricula. Yet this means to sophistication in a field of study may fall short of producing active scholars if the view of knowledge contained in it does not include a guarantee that the graduate will know what is most vital to his future learning — how to *question*.

College graduates can usually question at the simpler levels of intellection: "What is it? What does it do? How does it work?" At the upper reaches of questioning they are either confused or ignorant, not being able to phrase appropriately the questions, "Why does it work that way?" and, "How is it related to other things?" or the even more difficult question, "What is its significance?" College students need assistance with that kind of questioning.

This chapter started with the assertion that it is through *questioning*, not through *knowing*, that knowledge acquires its vitality. That assertion is an oversimplification, for questioning is a special case of knowing. It consists, in the main, of having learned how to ask the proper questions as well as the improper ones. It starts with, but goes far beyond, the learning of modes of questioning appropriate to a field of study. If it is creative, it penetrates the core of disciplined thought and dislocates some of the core elements. It is often disruptive. It is disinclined to hold steady and remain respectable.

If, as has been indicated, questioning or a sustained sense of inquiry must persist at every stage of education for a graduate to be educated in the fullest sense of the word, what then are the relationships that should exist between that which can be learned about questioning and that which can be learned about facts, concepts, generalizations, theories — the so-called content of education? Although the relationships between the two are not completely clear, a few clues to the connections between inquiry and content do exist.

As the first consideration, it needs to be noted that the problem we are dealing with in any discussion of questioning goes beyond cognition into the realm of affect. If the attitude established through formal learning is that creative questioning must follow the learning of answers to prefabricated questions, how do we enable the student in the advanced stages of his education to reverse that process? How do we move him or her to the cutting edge of knowledge? If his or herreaction to learning is unquestioning, it is most likely the result of habit — "Other people ask the questions and I try to give the answers."

It is evident that questioning cannot proceed in an intellectual vacuum. The questioner must know a great deal about a field of study to ask sophisticated questions. The moot point is, must he or she wait until he or she knows the field thoroughly before he or she begins his or her questioning? Must his or her initial questioning bear the hallmarks of sophistication characteristic of the expert, or should questioning begin at the earliest stages of study in a field and continue as one of the significant outcomes at every step along the way to scholarship? If the last question is to be answered in the affirmative, then written and oral examinations as well as classroom discourse in every field and at every level of study should give evidence of the ability of the student to pose significant questions. But instructors usually do not evaluate their students on ability to pose questions. Most often they evaluate answers to their own questions.

The second aspect of the relation of content to questioning is to be found in the stages through which inquiry appears to develop. Curiosity in the form of questioning is unsystematically induced through the culture; it is natural behavior for young children. The display of such curiosity disappears as a child proceeds through the school years. It is not that the student has ceased to inquire but that many of his or her questions either go unheeded or lie outside the formal structures which constitute the curricular apparatus. The student's questions no longer seem to fit within the systems of knowledge as his or her instructors conceive of them.

Poets, scientists, and other critical thinkers or questioners are probably shaped in their early years. The impact of formal education on their thinking has usually been less significant than the attitudes of inquiry they have brought to school. As creative thinkers, they are rarely encapsulated by systems or victimized by theories. Continuously they break out of the ordered thought of a discipline into new domains. Their attitudes of inquiry have been encouraged in childhood and sustained in youth.

A third clue is found in the informal evidence showing that students in college and graduate school have difficulty breaking out of routine patterns of thought in order to propose questions about what they have learned. Either they are intellectually hamstrung by formal systems or insufficiently acquainted with those systems to know the limitations that necessitate inquiry. The cognitive set accounting for their success in wrestling intellectually with teacher-made problems in their discipline may also account for their lack of success in going beyond these questions to those which they themselves pose.

Many teachers proceed on the assumption that the learner has much subject matter to learn, time is of the essence, and he or she must learn in a hurry. They conclude that the time-consuming procedure of fostering a student's inquiry and the scholarly pursuit of answers to his or her own questions is *inefficient*.

This argument proceeds from the limited view of efficiency that ignores the essential ingredient in any sound education — the ability to sustain education beyond school and college years by means of a sharpened sense of inquiry. If many of our graduates are incapable of an original *thought*, it may be that they have never learned to be capable of an original *question*.

A fourth factor is intelligence, or the lack of a sufficient amount of it in a number of students to enable them to go beyond the instructor's questions to their own inquiry. To be significant or challenging, the questions asked by a student must engage him or her in processes of *analysis, synthesis*, and *evaluation*.

Like poet and scientist, the essence of the student's creative questioning is relational; it must consist of attempting to comprehend the unlike in the like and the like in the unlike. According to Jacob Bronowski, such thinking is the basis for poem and scientific discovery. Since it requires a reasonably high level of intelligence, not many college or university students may be expected to startle their instructors with the creativity of their inquiry. For the others, nevertheless, it is essential that they engage, or attempt to engage, in that inquiry verging on the creative.

The rules of the game of questioning at the creative level are vague. It is true that some attempts have been made to standardize them, but the testimony of creative thinkers and studies in creativity of inquiry give warrant to the belief that it is not to be easily regimented. But the *freedom* to question, the *challenge* to question, the *leading* into questioning — these are essential. And the "whys," "as ifs," and "so whats" become more crucial types of questions than the "whats" and "hows."

The fifth and last consideration of how content and questioning may be related comes from scholars in a variety of disciplines but more particularly from psychologists, sociologists, and philosophers who have in recent years engaged in the study of knowledge in the disciplines and its relation to the curricula of public schools, colleges, and universities. These scholars have consistently made clear that the graduate of a discipline should be able to think like an expert in the field. They have indicated that in addition to knowledge about facts, concepts, theories, and issues, the student should be aware of the or she questions as yet unanswered in the or she field and should, as he or she advances, be increasingly more able to raise questions that stretch into the periphery of the discipline and even beyond it. Those teachers who include modes of inquiry for students learning the content of a discipline place insistent emphasis on the necessity to engage students in the intellectual processes representative of the ways in which experts in that field behave. A scholar in physics, for example, will therefore lead his or her students through the known and settled aspects of the field into the unknown, freeing them to ask the questions he or she already is asking, challenging them to search for answers in a responsible manner.

The nature of intellectual ferment in a classroom designed to promote student inquiry is such that the instructor will always feel ambiguous about who is in charge. As a matter of fact, no one is in charge. If the end sought is the *search* rather than the *found*, it soon becomes apparent that no person can be in charge in the usual sense.

What is really in charge is a way of *behaving toward learning* — an approach to a subject. Both the teacher and the taught are caught up in a mode of inquiry. The instructor becomes a *guide* to learning rather than the *authority* who dispenses questions and answers. The student becomes in large measure his or her own teacher because with the materials at hand, he or she must search for meanings and, in so doing, raise questions appropriate to the relationships he or she wishes to investigate.

No systematic inquiry has shown that graduates of such schooling would be any less informed about facts, concepts, generalizations, or theories than graduates of our classical system. There is evidence, however, that they would be more inventive, creative, and continuously curious. The difficulty with all such research is that it has never systematically directed its attention to student questioning over the range of all the school years. We need to continue to ask the proper questions about questioning.

For Further Reflection and Action ...

1. Do you really encourage student inquiry? Does your own questioning demonstrate vitality and creativity? What kind of example does your questioning set for students?

2. What are some of the best questions you have ever asked? What are some of the best questions your students have posed? Do you use some of those questions to stimulate students enrolled in your courses today?

3. How do our school systems thwart natural curiosity? Does your classroom extinguish the desire to learn? Why or why not? Have you seen classrooms that do? What are they like?

4. Do you believe student questions are as important as your questions? How do you communicate that message to your students?

5. What was your philosophy about questioning? How has it changed after reading this article? Will you continue to ask the proper questions about questioning?

Research Summary: Professors Part of the Problem?

Maryellen Weimer

Review of:
Barnes, Carol P. "Questioning in the College Classrooms."
Studies of College Teaching: Experimental Results,
Theoretical Interpretations, and New Perspectives.
Edited by Carolyn L. Ellner and Carol P. Barnes.
Lexington, MA: Lexington Books 1983, 61-81.

Faculty often blame students for a lack of participation and for passivity in class. Certainly students deserve some of that criticism. But research findings don't let faculty off the hook quite that easily.

In fact, research by Carol P. Barnes tends to support a much more difficult view. In her study of classroom questioning, Barnes found that faculty themselves contribute significantly to problems of non-participation.

Would you like to venture a guess as to the percentage of class time faculty devote to questioning? Did you guess something close to 3.65%? That's the mean percentage reported in this research, based on observations in 40 college classrooms. And no institutional type gets credit for a significantly higher percentage — not large or small public institutions, large private universities, or small private colleges.

But, you say, the percentage must vary by discipline, since some fields rely much more extensively on questioning. One would think

so, but that's not what this study found. The researcher compared
faculty in humanities/social sciences/arts with faculty in science/
engineering. Result: the percentage of time spent questioning by
each group failed to generate a statistically significant difference
between the means.

Well, you argue, certainly the percentage of questioning time must
change with the course level. After all, students first learn basic content and then they discuss, apply, synthesize, and evaluate in their
more advanced courses. Sorry, but this study didn't find that. Actually, more questioning occurred in the beginning courses — 3.99%,
compared with 3.30% in advanced courses.

Professors contribute to the problem of little participation by not
spending any significant amount of time asking students questions.
Is there a legitimate reason for that? Maybe professors have given
up asking questions because students never bother to answer.

We now have a chicken-egg dilemma on our hands. Who started it
can't be determined — and maybe it doesn't matter. The cause-effect
relationship as it now functions intensifies the problem. Students
don't answer, so professors don't ask. However, the power of the
teacher's position definitely puts him or her in a better place to do
something about the problem than the students.

Unfortunately, the problem gets complicated further by the kinds of
questions faculty ask. Barnes' research used a category system that
classified the questions into five types:

- *cognitive memory*, for recapitulative, clarifying, and
  factual questions
- *convergent thinking*, for questions of translation,
  association, explanation, and conclusion
- *divergent thinking*, in which questions asked students
  for responses that do things like elaborate, implicate,
  and synthesize
- *evaluative thinking*, in which answers must rate, judge,
  and qualify, among other things
- a catch-all category labeled *routine*, for questions
  pertaining to classroom management and for rhetorical
  and humorous questions

Almost 63% of all questions asked counted as *cognitive memory*
questions. The *divergent* and *evaluative* categories together accounted
for less than 5% of all the questions asked.

Quite bluntly, professors ask few questions that require students to think.

Asking simple, regurgitative questions extensively contributes to participation problems and inhibits learning. From the students' perspective, why bother answering, especially if the answer appears right there in the book or yesterday's notes? These questions make participation mundane, boring, and something you do so that you get the bonus participation points. You don't speak in class because you care or feel you have a legitimate contribution to make. Certainly, low-level questions have a place in the classroom. But should they occupy center stage as it appears they do?

The case against faculty includes still more damaging evidence. This study also looked at the *questioning patterns* of faculty, theorizing that what a professor does immediately before asking the question, coupled with the kind of question, might affect student participation.

Barnes considered 19 different questioning patterns. Five of these accounted for 61.5% of all faculty questioning patterns. Of this 61.5%, half fit into two patterns in which the professor lectured, asked a low-level (cognitive memory or convergent thinking) question, and then followed it with more lecture, either with (in the first pattern) or without (in the second) an interval of silence. In other words, 32% of all questioning patterns of college professors in this study elicited no student participation. In one of those two patterns there wasn't even an opportunity for it.

This study makes it difficult to let professors off the hook for participation problems. Barnes states the case bluntly:

> Our sense of mythology suggests that in college one would expect to find inquiring young minds being challenged by the intellectual and perceptive questions of learned professors. ... In this respect, the findings of this study were disappointing. Not only were many of the classes void of intellectual interchange between professors and students, but they also lacked excitement and vigor.

A strong indictment of our teaching methods. Then she adds, "One of the primary tools at the professor's disposal to infuse this atmosphere (of excitement and vigor) into his classroom is questioning, an age-old technique, but one which has not yet been tapped for its full potential." (79)

And I support that optimistic final conclusion. Making instructors aware of how they contribute to the problem is a large part of the solution. Few in our ranks would argue that on most days, more than 4% of the class time could be devoted to questioning. More challenging and thought-provoking questions can be prepared before class and raised a second day, if the first day brings no response.

And questioning patterns can be changed once we become aware of habituated sequences. In fact, increasing the effectiveness of questioning strategies rates as one of the easier ways to improve our pedagogical prowess.

For Further Reflection and Action ...

1. Estimate what percentage of time you devote to questioning. During the next two weeks, ask two or three students to record the amount of class time devoted to questioning and discussion.

2. What type of questions do you ask students? Listen to your own questions. In preparing your next discussion, see if you can't incorporate several questions from the divergent and evaluative thinking categories.

3. Are you aware of your own questioning patterns? Write a brief paragraph describing them. Have a colleague come to class and prepare a similar paragraph. How do the two compare?

Questioning
in the College Classroom

Ronald T. Hyman

College teachers share with all teachers an essential characteristic
— they ask questions. The question-answer dyad is central to the
thinking process and is therefore, essential to effective teaching. Indeed, it is impossible to conceive of a teaching situation in which
questions by the teacher and the students are not asked and answered. When teachers teach, they talk; when they talk, they ask
their students questions to stimulate thinking.

Purposes of Teacher Questions

A teacher might be able to accomplish most teaching through pedagogical techniques other than questioning. Asking questions, however, is a direct, sensible approach focused on the topic at hand. The
following list of purposes for questioning is descriptive and does not
imply approval. It merely illustrates some of the purposes teachers
have in mind when they pose questions:

- diagnose a student's degree or level of understanding of
  a concept, topic, etc.
- involve the student, help keep the student alert, and/or
  provide an opportunity for the student to shine in front
  of classmates
- test a student's knowledge and understanding and/or
  determine the extent to which supplied data can be used
  to reason and solve problems

- review, restate, and/or summarize fundamental points from previous sessions
- provide a springboard for discussion, stimulate creative imagination, and/or obtain ideas to which class members can react
- maintain discipline or stop a student from disrupting the class

Obviously, one question may serve two or more purposes simultaneously. A teacher may not be aware of all of his/her purposes in asking a particular question, and the results of the question may not be clear until the responses are analyzed in the context of the lesson. Student thinking is generally concentrated on the content of the teacher's question. Rarely does the student become aware of its multiple purposes.

It should be pointed out that purpose number 6 above differs significantly from the others listed. There is an important distinction to be made between asking a question to keep a student alert and involved and asking it as a tactic to embarrass a student who is disturbing the class, sleeping, reading a newspaper, or whatever. Such a tactic subverts the primary purpose of teacher questioning, which is to stimulate student thinking on a specific topic. A teacher is better advised to call for a student's attention in a straightforward way.

Since questioning is an essential teaching tool, it makes sense to use it to best advantage by learning about different types of questions, effective tactics for asking questions, strategies to guide question asking, methods for fielding student responses, and approaches for fielding student questions.

Types of Questions

The research literature on questioning offers several basic systems for categorizing questions according to the cognitive processes that the questions require the respondent to perform. In my opinion, the best system for categorizing questions in the college classroom is the eclectic one devised by Rodney P. Riegle (1976). Riegle lists three main types of questions:

1. *Interrogative questions:* those that request information, regardless of form

2. *Rhetorical questions:* those with an interrogative form but not an interrogative function (i.e., they do not request information)

3. *Ambiguous questions:* those that are functionally ambiguous (not clear whether they are interrogative or rhe or shetorical) or semantically ambiguous (not clear which of the interrogative subcategories is appropriate)

For the purposes of this chapter, only the categories for the Interrogative Questions are of importance. (See Table 1.)

Using Riegle's categories, it is possible to monitor and reflect upon the types of questions a teacher and his/her students ask.

For example, a teacher's questions may fall into a narrow range of categories. If the instructor is interested in developing in the students the ability to perform a wide range of cognitive processes, then the instructor will prepare and ask a variety of questions. Suppose a history teacher finds that he/she generally asks for causal (A1) explanations and only rarely for teleological (A2), functional (A3), or chronological (A5h) explanations. Once aware of this pattern, the teacher can begin to ask noncausal questions aimed at getting the students to offer noncausal explanations.

Examination of an instructor's questions may reveal ambiguity in wording or intent. For example, a teacher may intend to elicit different types of explanations, but may phrase questions in such a way that the students do not know what type of response is sought. Suppose the teacher asks, "Why did Argentina invade the Falkland Islands in the spring of 1982?" It is not clear whether this question seeks a causal, teleological, functional, or chronological explanation of the Argentines' action. Specifying the question clearly contributes to its effectiveness.

A teacher may be asking a broad range of questions and yet find that student questions are focused almost entirely on obtaining concrete examples of the items under study (A5b). This could indicate that students find the teacher's remarks abstract, difficult to understand, and lacking in the specifics they need for comprehension.

Examining student questions might show that students seldom ask each other for relationships (A5i). The instructor may need to take time to familiarize students with the variety of possible questions, provide models, and encourage practice so that students learn to broaden their questions during discussion.

Tactics for Questioning

Beyond the consideration of question type, there are several tactics suggested by the current literature that may assist teachers in improving the use of questioning in their teaching.

Table 1: Riegle's Question Classification System

Interrogative questions: Sentences with an interrogative function, regardless of form (i.e., requests for information)

A. *Empirical:* Questions about the world and our experiences of it

   1. *Causal:* Questions about the cause of something

     a. Why did the pond freeze?

     b. What caused World War I?

   2. *Teleological:* Questions about someone's purpose, aim, or goal

     a. Why did Nixon visit China?

     b. Why did our president choose Vancouver as the site of the 1976 PES Convention?

   3. *Functional:* Questions about something's function

     a. Why does the liver secrete bile?

     b. What is the function of the pancreas?

   4. *Non-normative judgment:* Requests for an estimate, prediction, ranking, or grading, but not value judgments

     a. How far is the green?

     b. Who will win the election?

     c. Is the second note higher or lower than the first?

   5. *Descriptive:* Requests for descriptions

     a. Requests for properties or characteristics.

       1. What color is it?
       2. What are the properties of iron?

     b. Requests for examples.

       1. What are some examples of homonyms?
       2. Give me a substance that dissolves in water.

     c. Requests for classifications.

       1. Is NaOH an organic or inorganic compound?
       2. What class of animals does the cat belong to?

     d. Requests for labels or names.

       1. Who is the President of France?
       2. Which part of the brain is the lowest?

     e. Requests for summaries.

       1. Summarize chapter three.
       2. What were the major points of this book?

     f. Requests for reviews.

       1. What have we said so far?
       2. What did the author say about ecology?

g. Requests for procedures or processes

    1. How is sulfur mined?

    2. How did you get the answer to this problem?

h. Requests for chronological sequences

    1. List in chronological order the events leading up to World War I.

    2. What sequence of events preceded Coolidge becoming President?

i. Requests for relationships

    1. What is the relationship between the Big Dipper and the North Star?

    2. How is spelling ability related to reading ability?

j. Requests for comparisons

    1. Compare Alabama to Auburn.

    2. What do these words have in common?

k. Requests for contrasts

    1. Contrast materialism with idealism.

    2. What is the difference between organic and inorganic compounds?

B. *Analytic:* Questions about the relationships among verbal, logical, or mathematical symbols

    1. *Linguistic:* Requests for definitions or the relationship between words

      a. Define "placid."

      b. What does "ambiguous" mean?

    2. *Logical:* Requests for the laws of logic or the relationship between logical symbols

      a. Why is this argument invalid?

      b. Does that conclusion follow?

    3. *Mathematical:* Requests for the laws of mathematics or the relationship between mathematical symbols

      a. What is 6×7?

      b. Why does angle A plus angle B equal 180 degrees?

C. *Normative judgment:* Requests for evaluations, obligatory judgments, or justifications

    1. Is Gerald Ford a good president?

    2. Should *Deep Throat* be banned?

D. *Preference:* Questions about likes and dislikes

    1. Do you like ice cream?

    2. Don't you like coming to school?

E. *Metaphysical:* Questions about supernatural beings, events, etc., that have no agreed upon method for arriving at an answer

    1. Does God exist?

    2. Why is there something rather than nothing?

Note: From Riegle (1976)

1. After asking a question, wait for a response. Do not answer the question yourself, repeat it, rephrase it, modify it, call on another student to answer it, or replace it with another question until you have waited at least three to five seconds. Students need time to think about the question and prepare their responses.

The research indicates that with a wait-time of three to five seconds, students respond more, increase the length and number of their responses, use complex cognitive processes, and begin to ask more questions. Sometimes, when teachers reword questions because they believe that the initial question is unclear, the result is greater student confusion. Students may not know which question to answer. (See Moriber 1971)

In another study, Mozer and Napell (1975) helped college physics teachers change their teaching behaviors. Increasing "wait-time" was one tactic emphasized. One teacher in that study said, "I tried to expand my "wait-time," and when students began to respond, I couldn't believe the misconceptions they'd held about some really basic concepts. If I hadn't allowed them time to speak up, I'd never have guessed at the gaps in their understanding of certain problems; I'd just have gone on talking over their heads until final exams."

In short, ask a question, wait, and thereby express your expectation to receive a response and your willingness to listen to it. *Be patient.*

2. Ask only one question at a time. Do not ask a string of questions one after the other in the same utterance. For example, ask, "Compare the skeleton of an ape with that of a human." Do not ask, "How are apes and man alike? Are they alike in bone structure and/or family structure and/or places where they live?" A series of questions tends to confuse students. They are not able to determine just what the teacher is requesting from them.

Napell (1978) states that videotape replays reveal an interesting pattern when the teacher asks a series of questions: "Hands will go up in response to the first question, and a few will go down during the second, and those hands remaining up gradually will get lower and lower as the instructor finally concludes with a question very different from the or she one for which the or she hands were initially raised."

Even if you believe that your question is unclear, *wait for a response.* You may find that students do indeed understand the question. By attempting to clarify, you may change the meaning of the question, thereby adding to the confusion.

Table 2: Resolving Value Conflicts

Questioner	*Respondent*
Q. What is the value conflict about?	*R.* Identifies and describes the conflict.
Q. What are the key words used in talking about this conflict?	*R.* Identifies central concepts.
Q. Define the key terms.	*R.* Defines essential terms for clarity of communication.
Q. What are the possible actions open to person X that will resolve the conflict? (What can person X do?)	*R.* Describes alternatives available.
Q. What are the likely consequences if person X took the first (second, third, etc.) alternative?	*R.* Predicts consequences of the various alternatives.
Q. What are the chances that the or shese consequences will occur?	*R.* Estimates the likelihood of consequences happening.
Q. Which consequences are good (desirable, preferred, advantageous) and which are not good?	*R.* Evaluates the consequences.
Q. What is or would be a similar, related conflict and its resolution?	*R.* Describes a parallel situation.
Q. Is there a general principle which indicates which value has priority over the other? If so, what is it?	*R.* Seeks overall ranking of values that will subsume this particular instance of conflict.
Q. At this point, what do you think person X should do to resolve the conflict?	*R.* Expresses resolution based on previous points.
Q. What are the reasons for resolving the conflict this way?	*R.* Gives reasons, justifies the suggested resolution to the value conflict.

Note: From Hyman (1979)

3. When student questions are desired, request them explicitly, wait, and then acknowledge student contributions. For example, a teacher may wish to solicit questions about the or she plays of Shakespeare that the class has been studying. The instructor might say, "Are there any questions or clarifications of points we have raised?" or "Please ask questions about the main characters or the minor characters, whichever you wish at this point," or, "In light of Sally's allusion to Lady Macbeth, I invite you to ask her some questions for embellishment or clarification."

Indicate to students that questions are not a sign of stupidity but rather the manifestation of concern and thought about the topic. Be very careful not to subtly or even jokingly convey the message that a student is stupid for asking for a clarification or restatement of an idea already raised in class or in the text.

4. Use a variety of probing and explaining questions. Ask questions that require different approaches to the topic, such as the causal, teleological, functional, or chronological questions given earlier. One way to begin is to avoid the words "why" and "explain" and to phrase your questions with words that give stronger clues about the type of explanation sought. Thus, for a chronological explanation, instead of asking, "Why did we have a depression in the 1930s?" try, "What series of events led to the stock market crash of 1929 and the high unemployment in the 1930s?"

A variety of probes can also be used to stimulate different cognitive processes. For example, suppose that a student in a sociology class has stated that the female's most important role in society is to be a mother. The teacher could probe that statement by asking, "Why do you say that?" However, it might be more stimulating to ask the student, or the class as a whole, "If you were Betty Friedan, Gloria Steinem, or Simone de Beauvoir, how would you react to that statement?" or, "What are the positive and negative consequences that arise within a family when a woman devotes herself chiefly to being a mother?" or, "What actions would you expect the government to take if and when it incorporated your idea into its social and economic policy?"

Strategies for Questioning

Beyond the tactics described above, questions need a strategic context or framework to enhance their meaning. An isolated question does not have the power that the same question has as the culmination of a sequence.

For example, consider the first illustrative question about the Falkland Islands. Suppose the teacher has asked and dealt with the responses to the following questions: According to Argentina, what is its historical claim to the Falklands? What previous attempts did Argentina and Britain make to settle their dispute? Who did Argentina believe would support its action? What did Argentina believe would be Britain's reaction to the invasion?

Now, suppose you ask, seeking a *functional* explanation, "What function, then, did the invasion serve for Argentina?" This question has impact because it is an outgrowth of the previous four questions. There is a synergistic and cumulative effect when the five connected questions are asked together. The students need to consider the responses to the previous questions when they offer their explanation of the invasion of the Falklands by the Argentines. Their explanation is enhanced by accounting for the data presented in the previous responses. Their cognitive processes are stimulated as they grasp the direction the series of questions is taking.

The best context for a given question is a questioning strategy. A questioning strategy is *a carefully planned sequence of major questions designed to achieve a teaching goal.* The careful planning eliminates confusing gaps between questions and assures the inclusion of complementary questions that provide helpful insights, variety, and spice to the discussion.

Obviously, questioning strategies must be formulated ahead of time, since it is virtually impossible to do so in the midst of the fast-paced, active, and complex interaction in the classroom. By planning ahead, the teacher can better determine the progression of questions that serve as a model of logical thinking for the students.

Table 2 offers a general questioning strategy for resolving value conflicts. Conflict occurs when a person must choose between equally important values. As the first step in this strategy the respondents must identify and describe the conflict at hand. This may appear to be simple, but it often takes time for students to pinpoint just where the conflict resides. It is essential that the teacher seek several responses to this question.

If there is difficulty in this first step, it may help to proceed to the next two steps, identifying and defining the key terms, and then to return to the identification of the conflict. Once the key terms are known, it is often easier to decide just what the conflict is.

The general strategy should be modified and made applicable to the specific conflict under consideration. As the strategy is prepared, it is helpful to do two things:

- Prepare a right-hand column similar to the one in Table 2 to serve as a check on the logic. By scanning the right column it is possible to check the cognitive processes required to see if they progress logically and if they lead toward the teacher's goal. This can also serve as a check on the range of question types being prepared.

- Prepare alternative ways to phrase some of the complex questions.

Attention to tactics and strategies enhances the effectiveness of the teacher's questions. Questions become a reliable means to stimulate student thought. For more specific help with tactics and strategies for interacting with students, see *Strategic Questioning* (Hyman 1979) and *Improving Discussion Leadership* (Hyman 1980).

Tactics for Fielding Student Responses

One natural outcome of teacher questioning is student responding. It is important to attend to students' responses. The ways in which the instructor fields student responses will influence future responses. There are many options open to the teacher after a student response, and there is no pedagogical rule mandating a particular behavior on the teacher's part.

Nevertheless, one need not be a psychologist to realize that it is helpful to reinforce good responses. Students look to the instructor for guidance and support. If the instructor ignores them or shows virtual indifference, student behavior may be inhibited even if it is appropriate. Chastised students, and especially those who feel humiliated, may become so angry or fearful that they will refuse to respond in the future.

The goal, then, is for the instructor to field responses in such a way that the quantity and quality of future responses are enhanced. The following are several tactics for fielding responses. Please keep in mind that these tactics do not indicate how to field all types of responses under all conditions.

1. Praise the student in a strong, positive way for a correct or excellent response. Use such terms as "excellent answer," "absolutely correct," and "bull'seye." These terms are quite different from the common mild phrases teachers often use, such as "OK," "hm-hm," and "all right." Especially when the response is long, the teacher should try to find at least some part that deserves strong praise and then comment on it.

2. Make comments pertinent to the specific student response. For example, suppose that a student has offered an excellent response to the question, "What function did the invasion serve for Argentina?" The instructor might say, "That was excellent, Pat. You included national political reasons as well as mentioning the Argentine psychological drive to become the South American leader." This response gives an excellent rating to the student in an explicit and strong form. It also demonstrates that the instructor has listened carefully to the student's response by supplying comments specific to the student's ideas.

3. Make no comment at all after each specific response within a series of responses to a single question; make a general comment after the series of responses is complete. Suppose the teacher has asked the sequence of questions above on the Argentine invasion of the Falklands. Before asking the final question, the teacher could designate three students to respond. The teacher could then nod or point to each in turn to supply answers. After the third response the teacher might say, "Those were excellent answers; the first emphasized national political functions, while the second and third concentrated on the psychological factors for Argentina within South America and in the world at large."

There are at least two good reasons for using this tactic to field multiple responses. First, the teacher's comments have the tendency to shift the focus of discourse back to the teacher. By nodding or pointing to the next student, the instructor keeps the focus on the students' response. Second, and most important, if the instructor praises the first student immediately, the second student is likely to pick up the message that the teacher expects an answer similar to the first one. The second student will hesitate to go off on another tack even though it may be a good one.

It is very important that the teacher keep track of the responses in the series so that they can be reinforced at the end. Fielding the responses in this way encourages each student's own particular response. It also helps students learn that they do not need to have the teacher's comments after each of their responses.

4. Build on the student's response. If the instructor continues to discuss a point after a student's response, he/she should try to incorporate the key elements of the response into the discussion. By using the student's response, the teacher shows that he or she values the points made. By referring to the student explicitly by name (e.g., "As Pat pointed out, the Falklands national political status..."), the teacher gives credit where credit is due.

5. Avoid the "Yes, but ..." reaction. Teachers use "Yes, but..." or its equivalent when a response is wrong or at least partly wrong. The overall impact of these phrases is negative and deceptive even though the teacher's intent is probably positive. The "Yes, but" fielding move says the response is correct or appropriate with one breath and then takes away the praise with the next breath. Some straightforward alternatives can be recommended:

   a. Wait to a count of five with the expectation that another student will volunteer a correct or better response.

   b. Ask, "How did you arrive at that response?" (Be careful, however, not to ask this question only when you receive inadequate responses. Ask it also at times when you receive a perfectly good response.)

   c. Say, "You're right regarding X and that's great; wrong regarding Y. Now we need to correct Y so that we can get everything correct."

   d. Say, "Thanks. Is there someone else who wants to respond to the question or comment on the response we've already heard?"

These four alternatives are obviously not adequate to fit all cases. Indeed, it is generally difficult to field wrong or partially wrong responses because students are sensitive to teacher criticism. However, with these four alternatives as examples, an instructor will probably be able to generate others as needed.

Tactics for Fielding Student Questions

Strange as it may seem, many college teachers are ill at ease when students ask them questions. For some reason, they have not learned to field questions. Fielding is a broader concept than responding: responding to a question is but one fielding option. The skill of fielding student questions is vital for a teacher who wants students to think about the topic under study; one result of student thinking is student questioning.

If there are few student questions, it may be that students are not attending to the teacher's remarks and not thinking about the topic at hand. Alternatively, students may be afraid to ask questions because they think they will be put down. It is also possible that students do not ask questions because they believe that the teacher doesn't want them to ask questions. That is, the teacher somehow discourages students from asking questions.

This discouragement is rarely explicit; few teachers actually say, "Don't ask me any questions." (They may say, "Hold your questions for a few minutes.")

Generally, the discouragement is implicit. It comes from the negative way a teacher fields a student question. For example, "We discussed that issue yesterday," or, "That question is not really on target." Sometimes an instructor will answer the student's question and then say something like, "Where were we before we got sidetracked?" After one of these negative fielding moves, a student may say, "I'll never ask another question in this class."

It is difficult to explain why teachers discourage student questions in this way. However, some tentative reasons can be offered.

- Teachers feel the need to be in control, both of the content and of the procedures in the classroom.

- Teachers feel they need to "cover" the established course content. Time is precious; there is never enough of it to cover the material. Thus, they discourage student questions because the questions may lead them away from their material.

- Teachers also want to appear knowledgeable to their students. Student questions may embarrass the instructor who is unable to respond adequately.

In short, instructors fear that they may lose control or lose face if students ask questions. The potential for loss of control and loss of face is real. It surely is possible for a teacher to go off track and to appear to lack knowledge. However, it is also true that the fear of this happening is overdrawn and the probability for it to occur is low.

The teacher must weigh the advantages gained by permitting and encouraging questions against the need to maintain tight control in order to be sure to cover the material and to appear knowledgeable. (In this author's experience, the advantages of student questions far outweigh the risks.)

Some tactics for fielding student questions in a positive way are in order. Again, these tactics do not suit all cases. They are simply examples of the options available.

1. Praise the student for asking a question. For example, "Thanks for asking that," or, "That's a good question," or, "That's an insightful question that everyone can consider." These are simple reactions, and yet few teachers reinforce students for asking questions. College students need this reinforcement because their previous experience has generally led them to the conclusion that student questions are not valued.

2. Answer the student's question directly as often as possible. Students ask questions because they legitimately seek a response. They do not ask questions, by and large, to be cute or disruptive. Moreover, they want a response from the teacher. Do not play games with the student by asking a question in return or by stalling. By responding directly, the teacher indicates that the question is worthwhile.

Teachers often deflect questions to other students or to the class in general. Students generally want the teacher to respond directly. If the instructor wants to hear first what other students have to say, the "deflecting" move can be prefaced with something like, "After we hear what some students have to say, then I'll offer my answer, too," or, "I'm asking Joe to respond specifically since he is the expert on this particular topic. If you still want my response when Joe is finished, just let me know." In this way, the questioner is informed of the instructor's strategy and does not assume that the question is being avoided or discounted by the deflection to another student.

3. Let the student know if a question leads into a new area. If a student question prompts an instructor to launch into a new topic, the plan should be indicated to the class. For example, "That's an excellent question and it deserves further exploration. To do so, let's shift to topic X. I think you will see the response develop. If not, please ask again. Thanks." While this does not satisfy the student with an immediate and direct response, the teacher does indicate that the question is valued, both explicitly through praise and implicitly by involving the student in the plans.

Summary

The question-answer dyad in the college classroom is a critical teaching element. It is critical when the teacher is questioner and the student respondent, and it is especially so when the roles are reversed. To achieve the multiple purposes served by questions, an instructor can:

- use a variety of different question types to stimulate the students' cognitive processes
- use appropriate tactics in asking questions
- formulate questioning strategies
- field the students' responses positively

An instructor can promote student questioning by fielding questions in an encouraging, reinforcing manner. All of these suggestions can be helpful in making the student an active participant in classroom interaction and in stimulating student thinking.

References

Hyman, Ronald T. *Improving Discussion Leadership.* New York: Teachers College Press 1980.

Hyman, Ronald T. *Strategic Questioning.* Englewood Cliffs, NJ: Prentice-Hall 1979.

Moriber, G. "Wait-Time in College Science Classes." *Science Education,* 55 (1971), 321-328.

Mozer, F.S., and Napell, S.M. "Instant Replay and the Graduate Teaching Assistant." *American Journal of Physics,* 43 (1975), 242-244.

Napell, S.M. "Using Questions to Enhance Classroom Learning." *Education,* 99 (1978) 188-197.

Riegle, Rodney P. "Classifying Classroom Questions." In Kenneth A. Strike (Ed.), *Philosophy of Education.* Urbana, IL: Philosophy of Education Society 1976.

For Further Reflection and Action ...

1. Can you think of a question that fulfills more than one of the six purposes listed by Hyman? Have you ever used a question to embarrass a disruptive student? How effective was the strategy? Has a student ever used a question to embarrass you or challenge your authority? How effective was the strategy?

2. How often do you attempt to begin a discussion with "why" or "explain"? Think of a few examples and modify them to more accurately stimulate the type of cognitive process desired.

3. Using the questioning strategy as outlined in Table 2, find a colleague and practice questioning sequences. What kinds of patterns evolved? In what ways is it helpful to examine question progressions?

4. How do you respond to the answers given by students? Are you positive? negative? indifferent? Review Hyman's five tactics for fielding student responses and incorporate them, as needed, into your own responses.

5. Do you use any of Hyman's three suggested tactics for fielding students' questions? Are the tactics effective for you? Are there any other strategies that you might employ when responding to students' questions?

6. Will the strategies proposed in this chapter make students think? Whyor why not?

Planning Questions

Stephanie Goodwin and colleagues

Effective questioning sessions in classrooms require advance preparation. While some instructors may be skilled in extemporaneous questioning, many find that such questions have phrasing problems, are not organized in a logical sequence, or do not require students to use the desired thinking skills. Below are some steps and suggestions for planning questions.

1. *Decide on your goal or purpose for asking questions.* Your goal should help you determine what levels of questions you will ask.

2. *Select the content for questioning.* Choose material that you consider important rather than trivial. Students will study and learn based on the questions you ask. Do not mislead them by emphasizing less important material.

3. *Phrase your questions carefully.*
   - Ask questions that require an extended response or at least a "content" answer. Avoid questions that can be answered "yes" or "no" unless you are going to follow with more questions to explore reasoning.
   - Phrase your questions so that the task is clear to students. Questions such as, "What about foreign affairs?" do not often lead to productive answers and discussion. "What did we say about chemical bonding?" is too general unless you are seeking only a review of any material the students remember.

- Be sure the questions allow enough flexibility so that students are not playing a guessing game. Avoid "guess what I am thinking" questions.

Example:

Instructor: What is a symptom of Multiple Sclerosis?

Student 1: Numbness.

Instructor: What else?

Student 2: Tingling.

Instructor: What else?

Student 3: Blurred vision.

Instructor: I'm thinking of a different one.

Student 4: Slurred speech.

Instructor: OK, that's the one I was looking for. Let's go on from there ....

- Your questions should not contain the answers. Avoid implied response questions when you are genuinely seeking an answer from the class. A question such as, "Don't we all agree that the author of the article exaggerated the dangers of Agent Orange to strengthen his or her viewpoint?" will not encourage student response.

4. When planning your questions, *try to anticipate possible student responses.* You might do this by considering:

- What are some typical misconceptions that might lead students to incorrect answers?
- Am I asking an open or closed question?
- What type of response do I expect from students? A definition? An example? A solution?
- Will I accept the answer in the student's language or am I expecting the textbook's words or my own terms?
- What will my strategy be for handling incorrect answers?
- What will I do if students do not answer?

Anticipating student responses should help in your planning by forcing you to consider whether phrasing is accurate, whether questions focus on the goal you have in mind, and whether you have enough flexibility to allow students to express ideas in their own words.

5. Until you are quite skilled at classroom questioning you should *write your main questions in advance.* Arrange your list in some logical sequence (specific to general, lower level to higher level, a sequence related to content).

Should you think of additional or better questions during the questioning process, you can be flexible and add those or substitute them for some of your planned questions. However, having a prepared list of questions will help to assure that you ask questions appropriate for your goals and representative of the important material.

For Further Reflection and Action ...

1. Do you "plan" questions? How? Why should you?

2. Pull out a set of lecture notes that you have recently taught. Carefully follow the five steps outlined in this reading to develop the important points of the material.

3. Having thoroughly planned the questions for this lecture, did you discover new directions for development of content material? Will you be better prepared to stimulate interest in the topic? to organize your own thoughts and presentation? to field questions on related areas?

4. Use a couple of "planned" questions in class. Does the quality of the question affect the quality of the answer?